MINK COATS DON'T TRICKLE DOWN

The Economic Attack on Women and People of Color

Randy Albelda

Elaine McCrate

Edwin Meléndez

June Lapidus

SOUTH END PRESS
THE CENTER FOR POPULAR ECONOMICS

first edition, first printing
cover design and production by Nick Thorkelson
text design and production by Ellen Herman and the South End Press collective
printed in the U.S.A.

ISBN 0-89608-328-4

Library of Congress Catalog Card Number: 87-63363
Mink coats don't trickle down: the economic attack on women and people of color / Randy Albelda...[et al.].
  1. United States—Economic Policy—1981- 2. United States—Economic Conditions—1981- 3. Supply-side economics—United States. 4. Women—United States—Economic conditions. 5. Afro-Americans—Economic conditions. I. Albelda, Randy Pearl. II. Economic report of the people.
  HC106.8.M57 1988   87-36939
  338.973—dc19   CIP

South End Press, 116 St. Botolph St., Boston, MA 02115

TABLE OF CONTENTS

ACKNOWLEDGMENTS, page 4

CHAPTER 1, page 5

Scarcely Allocating Resources

Economic Policies of the Rich and Famous...Fed Up...On Our Backs...To Market, To Market...Is It Trickling Down?

CHAPTER 2, page 11

Are You Better Off Today...?

Social Dissolution...Income Stagnation and Inequality...Are Baby Boomers to Blame?...Family Revolution...Economic Dislocation...Government Retrenchment...Can We Do Better?

CHAPTER 3, page 25

Reaganomics and Racial Inequality

The New Age of Reaction...The Reversal of a Decade of Economic Gains for People of Color...Does the Market Promote Racial Equality?...Reconstructing the Racial Order...The Assault on Affirmative Action...The Politics of Race

CHAPTER 4, page 41

Women and Children Last

Women Hold Up Half the Economy (At Less Than Half the Price)...Government Off Whose Backs?...Women and Children Last...The New Double Standard...Impoverished Freedoms

NOTES, page 55

ABOUT THE AUTHORS, page 63

ACKNOWLEDGMENTS

This book is a revised and updated version of Chapters 3, 4, and 5 of the *Economic Report of the People* written by the Center for Popular Economics and published by South End Press in 1986. While only the authors of the revised chapters are listed on the cover of this book, everyone from the Center for Popular Economics deserves credit and thanks, in particular Sam Bowles and Lyuba Zarsky, the initial editors and Nancy Folbre, graph maker *par excellence*. Thanks as well to Karin Aguilar-San Juan who provided help with graphics, Mona Kotch who patiently typed the manuscript, and Ellen Herman, our editor at South End Press.

Many people served as consultants to the project, too many to list here. But we would like to thank CPE's funders who make all our work with activists and popular economists across the United States and Canada possible. The original project was made possible by the generous support of the Field Foundation, the Presbyterian Church (U.S.A.), the United Church of Christ, Board of Homeland Ministries, and the Economics and Democratic Values Project.

We would also like to thank all the foundations and individuals who have enabled us to continue our economics education work over the years: A Territory Resource; Bread and Roses Community Fund; Circle Fund; Discount Foundation; The Domestic and Foreign Missionary Society of the Protestant Episcopal Church in the U.S.A.; Evergreen Exchange/National Community Funds; Haymarket Peoples Fund; Holy Cross Fathers; Max and Anna Levinson Foundation; The Limantour Fund; Peace Development Fund; Public Concern Foundation; PBP Foundation; Shalan Foundation; The Sunflower Foundation; The Fairtree Foundation; Twenty-first Century Foundation; Windom Fund; Women's Opportunity Giving Fund of the Presbyterian Church in the U.S.A.; and The Youth Project.

CHAPTER 1

Scarcely Allocating
Resources

Eight years of Ronald Reagan and the triumph of conservative economic policies have changed the American people and the U.S. economy. Trickle-down economics with its emphasis on military spending, borrowing from the future, and cutting social services has left the domestic economy and the majority of workers and families defenseless. Roads go unbuilt; hospital beds lie empty waiting for the rich while the poor and uninsured wait in the lobbies below; teachers teach without books in run-down schools; and across the nation more and more people live on the streets.

The recent revival of free-market orthodoxy represents a deliberate attempt to dismantle the economic order which emerged from the Great Depression and World War II. When the postwar boom ended in the early 1970s, conservative economists and business interests mounted an attack on the legacy of the New Deal and Great Society. Since 1979, the architects of a new economic reaction—at the Federal Reserve Board, in conservative think tanks, and since 1981 in the Oval Office—have dedicated themselves to the task of turning back the clock.

• Economic Policies of the Rich and Famous

Reagan's philosophy and strategy rest on three primary pillars. The first is the belief that throwing money at the rich and into the hands of big business is the key to economic growth and investment. This is called "supply-side" or "trickle-down" economics. The second is a concerted policy to "spend and borrow" in order to fund a military complex and pare away resources from social and human investments. The last pillar of the conservative agenda is free-market rhetoric which

5

warns that when government intervenes in the marketplace, inefficiencies and unfairness result.

• Fed Up

Supply-side economics predicts that production will increase when producers have the economic incentives to do so. In other words, give investors easy credit, promise high rates of return, and the benefits will soon trickle down to the rest of us through more jobs, goods, and services. The efforts of the Federal Reserve Board in 1979 were intended to do more than start the trickle. Paul Volcker, then Chairman of the Federal Reserve, initiated a rapid decrease in the money supply. The lack of available money sent the price of money (interest rates) soaring. The result was higher rates of return on money lent to the banks but also a high premium for those who borrowed. Inflation quickly subsided but unemployment soared as businesses which borrowed money in order to produce found the price too high. Unemployment increased to the highest level since the 1930s, wages fell, and workers' ability to bargain was weakened.

The rise in interest rates meant that people around the world with money to lend found U.S. interest rates very appealing. In order to put money in U.S. banks, foreign investors had to convert it to dollars, thereby driving the demand for dollars up and with it the price of the dollar relative to other currencies. As the price of the dollar rose, so did the price of U.S. goods abroad, meaning fewer exports. The level of imports rose since the dollar could buy more foreign goods. As a result, the U.S. trade deficit—the amount of exports minus the amount of imports—has risen tremendously, representing an outflow of dollars from the U.S. economy. The only way to pay for this outflow is through borrowing. Recently, the value of the dollar has fallen but the trade deficit has barely responded.

• On Our Backs

The winning slogan of the 1980 election was "Get government off the backs of the American people." Since 1980, government spending has actually increased considerably but not through old-fashioned methods like taxes. Instead, Reaganomics has stocked the kitty and diverted it to military endeavors by borrowing the money from rich people and rewarding them handsomely with interest payments. Spending increases for education, health, human services, and other social investments have been reversed and in some cases funds for programs decreased or were eliminated.

Some important changes have resulted from the "guns rather than butter" strategy. The national deficit has ballooned. The Reagan administration has mortgaged away our future. If the U.S. government

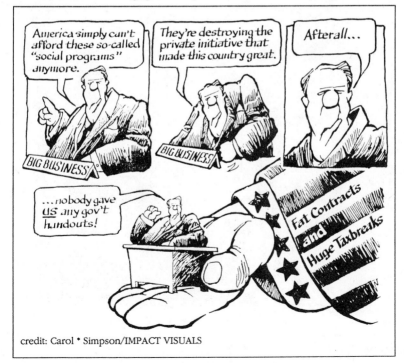

credit: Carol • Simpson/IMPACT VISUALS

were buying investments today that would yield high returns in the future, the American people might benefit. But what we are buying is a foreign policy that has antagonized enemies and allies alike, a star wars defense system that can't defend the population, and military equipment that doesn't work.

By default, the feds have left social policy to the states. Welfare, health insurance, education, and health care services have lost federal priority. Individual states are left to pick up the pieces. Those states on the gold coasts, with the most resources, fight over scarce state revenues while the vast interior is left to do without.

UNCLE SAM TALKS TOUGH WITH TODAY'S TEENS.

credit: Ken Brown

"Spend and borrow" fiscal policy is really an income redistribution scheme that never resorts to tax reform. Spending away from low- and moderate-income families while borrowing from the rich assures a Robin Hood in reverse Hollywood script ending: the rich get richer. The top corporate military contractors receive above-average profits which are then turned around to subsidize their non-military production.

• To Market, To Market

If government is not providing social goods, then how are they to be allocated? The conservative economic agenda relies heavily on the market to set the course. In reality, of course, the government gets off some backs and not others. With lucrative military contracts, bank bailouts, and a deliberately overvalued dollar, the Reagan administration has played a major role in determining which industries and communities thrive—and which are abandoned to the slash-and-burn logic of free-market competition.

The Iran-Contra connection highlights the extent to which the administration places its trust in the marketplace: private arms sales *are* foreign policy. Deregulation has been the watchword of the 1980s but has played havoc in both the banking and transportation (particularly passenger airlines) industries. Vast investments have been made in mergers and acquisitions but very little in new productive equipment and machinery. Workers face fewer jobs and restructuring of the workplace while consumers receive fewer services at the same or higher prices.

In labor markets, the administration has allowed discrimination to thrive by dismantling affirmative action and pooh-poohing initiatives like comparable worth. The throwback to an era gone by is exemplified by leaving civil rights to be violated by the marketplace rather than adjudicated in the courts.

The stock market "crash" in the fall of 1987 exposes the fragility of an economy precariously buoyed by paper investment and double deficits. Without the sound economic base of investment in new facilities, the meteoric rise of stock prices has come tumbling down. Rather than sounding the rallying cry of increased production in the kinds of goods and services that are needed by working people and would bolster the economy, the Reagan administration, Congress, and 1988 presidential hopefuls are all hawking increased austerity measures as sure-fire solutions. Wall Street investors hope to shift their losses onto the backs of poor and working people.

• Is It Trickling Down?

This pamphlet examines exactly how trickle-down economic policies have affected the standard of living of most Americans, especially people of color and women. Rather then restoring economic prosperity, eight years of Reagan have profoundly reversed gains made through the efforts of the civil rights, labor, and women's movements over the last thirty years. Claims of an economic recovery and vast growth in employment are masked by the lack of productive investment and the inability of many to support themselves and their families in low-wage, dead-end service sector jobs. Concerted policy decisions and deterioration caused by the marketplace have generated only one thing among the poor and working poor—more poverty.

CHAPTER 2

Are You Better Off Today...?

Thirty-five years old and divorced, Mary worked a full-time sales job in a Philadelphia department store to support herself and her two sons. At the minimum wage, her take-home pay came to $540 per month—below the poverty line. Until the fall of 1981, Mary received a $169 monthly check from Aid to Families with Dependent Children. But on October 1, 1981, the welfare check stopped coming. Like 400,000 other poor working parents, Mary became ineligible for assistance under the Reagan administration's budget reforms. Along with her welfare check, Mary's family lost its health insurance under the Medicaid program.[1]

On March 30, 1984, a mock funeral procession gathered in South Chicago. Composed of steelworkers, many with over twenty-five years of experience in the South Works of U.S. Steel, the procession marked the shutdown of the plant. The neighbors of these workers, laid-off when Wisconsin Steel shut down four years earlier, had few words of encouragement to offer them. One of them, a black man in his forties, had gone on to do odd jobs like installing bathtubs and fixing gutters. Another, a Chicano in his fifties, spent his days looking for aluminum cans and flattening them out.[2]

The gap between America's rich and poor is growing wider. According to the U.S. Census Bureau:

- the poorest 40 percent of the population received only 15.5 percent of the total national income in 1986, less than in any year since data were initiated in 1947, and less than the richest 5 percent. The wealthiest 20 percent captured 43.7 percent of all income, the highest proportion on record (see Figure 2.1)[3];
- the income gap between blacks and whites has barely budged and widened between Latinos and whites between 1979 and 1985. Black households earned on average 63.9 percent of what white households

did in 1985, only slightly higher than the 63.7 percent figure in 1979. Hispanic household income in 1985 was 72.1 percent of white household income, a drop from 77.1 percent in 1979[4];

- poverty rates among children under eighteen rose from 16 percent in 1979 to 20.2 percent in 1986. Over half the children in families with a female head of household lived in poverty in 1986.[5]

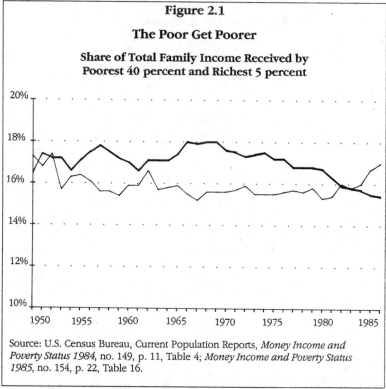

Figure 2.1

The Poor Get Poorer

Share of Total Family Income Received by Poorest 40 percent and Richest 5 percent

Source: U.S. Census Bureau, Current Population Reports, *Money Income and Poverty Status 1984*, no. 149, p. 11, Table 4; *Money Income and Poverty Status 1985*, no. 154, p. 22, Table 16.

Today's increasing income inequality is the result of long-term structural changes, especially the shift from manufacturing to services and the erosion of marriage as a social institution. But unlike government policies in the 1960s and 1970s, conservative economic policies since 1979 have not attempted to counter these social and economic trends by redistributing income toward the poor. Indeed, conservative policies have halted improvements in average U.S. living standards and increased income disparities between people of color and whites, children and adults, rich and poor.

• Social Dissolution

The United States is currently undergoing a major breakdown in its system of distributing and redistributing income on a scale reminiscent of the Great Depression. This breakdown stems from three developments.

First, the social institution of marriage is eroding. An unprecedented growth in the number of households maintained by women has undermined the most effective system of redistributing income from one person to another in the United States—the married-couple family. While more women have entered the labor force in the postwar economy, they and their children have in general not made up in earned income what they lost in shared income with men. Women remain largely ghettoized in low-paying clerical and service jobs and women's wages remain considerably lower than men's (see Chapter 4).

Second, the U.S. economy has suffered a long-term decline in its overall performance. Predating the Volcker-Reagan strategy of conscious "trickle-down" policies, economic decline precipitated the downward slide in incomes and heightened pre-existing trends toward greater inequality. Some of this decline is directly associated with economic stagnation between 1973 and 1979: gains in real wages and growth in the real per capita value of most government transfers ground to a halt in the 1970s.

These trends are associated with the rapid growth of service industries throughout the postwar period. With fast food establishments at one end and financial services at the other, the service sector is often characterized by lower wages, less full-time work, bigger wage gaps between workers, and less union protection than in manufacturing industries.

The third development contributing to income stagnation and inequality has been the deliberate application of conservative economic policy since 1979. Macroeconomic policy and changes in the tax and transfer systems under Volcker and Reagan have not improved living standards. These policies actually reduced disposable income for 60 percent of the entire population. The real winners were the richest 20 percent.

Throughout the 1970s, government redistribution programs softened the impact of the economic crisis and the revolution in family structure. Sub-employment and rising unemployment were offset by rising government transfers. But the public income maintenance system was ill prepared to wage full-scale war against the poverty and inequality resulting from the shortfall of job opportunities and the demise of the male breadwinner family. In the 1980s, poor economic perfor-

mance and high unemployment, coupled with massive retrenchment in the government's earlier commitment to redistribute income toward the bottom, fueled the explosion of poverty and inequality.

• Income Stagnation and Inequality

Free-market advocates claim that the market is the cure for economic inequality. They point to the post-1982 recovery as proof of renewed progress for the majority of U.S. citizens. The new economic orthodoxy, conservatives assert, has ushered in an era of economic opportunity for all Americans. By eliminating "nonessential" and "ineffective" government programs, Washington claims to have provided the necessary incentive for people to work, save, and invest—to be productive, and to be rewarded for it.

In reality, conservative economics has slowed the improvement in the standard of living. Adjusted for inflation, U.S. after-tax per capita income grew only 0.9 percent per year from 1979 to 1986. This was a substantial decrease from average annual growth rates of 3.3 percent between 1959 and 1969, and it was virtually no improvement over growth rates of 0.8 percent between 1973 and 1979.[6]

The civilian unemployment rate averaged over 7 percent between 1984 and 1986. This is higher than the level of unemployment in any previous cyclical peak since the Great Depression. Workers of color were hit especially hard. With unemployment at 14 percent, one out of eight black workers over twenty years of age was officially counted as unemployed in 1986.[7] This official unemployment rate actually underestimates the number of people without jobs because it does not include people who have simply given up looking for jobs, or people who are involuntarily employed part-time.

Conservative economics also reversed progress toward closing income disparities between the rich and poor. The gap between the incomes of rich and poor families narrowed substantially in the twenty years between the late 1940s and the late 1960s; it then widened gradually over the 1970s. In the 1980s, it exploded.[8] By 1986, the percentage share of aggregate family income received by the most affluent 5 percent of families had risen to 17 percent, its highest level since 1961. The richest 20 percent also gained, while the share of the poorest 20 percent fell to 4.6 percent.[9]

Meanwhile, the super-rich maintained their privileged position. In 1983, the 2 percent of all families who owned financial assets such as savings and government bonds held over half of such assets; the top 10 percent held 86 percent of the assets.[10] Because information on asset ownership is one of the best kept secrets in the U.S. economy—data is only sporadically available—it is not possible to determine precisely how the fortunes of the very wealthy have changed over the last few decades. But we can conclude that a tiny minority of families continues to own and ultimately control the lion's share of non-labor economic resources.

The human misery of declining or stagnating income cannot be measured quantitatively. But a few key indicators, such as poverty and infant mortality rates present evidence of staggering costs. After 1978, poverty rates increased among young men, prime-age men, female-headed households, children, whites, blacks, and Latinos. Poverty rates increased at a particularly rapid clip from 1980 to 1983. Economic expansion since 1983 has reduced the official poverty rate slightly, but the 1986 rate was just under 18 percent higher than in 1979, after the late 1970s business cycle expansion, and close to 25 percent higher than in 1973, after the expansion of the early 1970s.[11]

One of the most poignant and widely accepted indicators of the standard of living is the infant mortality rate. This rate has declined rapidly over the years in the United States and in other economically developed countries. But in 1984, according to provisional data, the

A Working Economy for Americans/cpf

U.S. infant mortality rate decline slowed to a barely perceptible crawl.[12] Some analysts attribute this disturbing setback to cuts in federal funding for programs for pregnant women, young children, and mothers of young children.[13]

In some places, infant mortality rates actually rose during the early 1980s. According to a 1985 study of the rural poor, aggregate infant mortality rates in the eighty-five poorest rural counties rose significantly between 1981 and 1983. This gap in infant mortality rates between the rural poor and the rest of the nation grew by a dramatic 39 percent in these two years.[14] Furthermore, the gap between black and white infant mortality rates grew by 4 percent from 1982 to 1983. Black infants died at nearly double the rate of white infants in 1983.[15]

Some observers attribute regional and racial discrepancies in the rate of infant death to high rates of unemployment. For example, after a thirty-year decline, the infant mortality rate in Michigan rose by 3 percent between 1980 and 1981. For thirty-seven consecutive months during that period, Michigan suffered double digit unemployment. Particularly hard hit were Flint and Pontiac counties, where the unemployment rate was over 26 percent in December 1982. The rate of infant deaths in each of these two counties was twice the state average.[16]

• Are Baby Boomers to Blame?

Some economists argue that the apparent deterioration in the standard of living is primarily the result of the large influx of baby boomers into the labor force in the 1970s. According to this view, the entry-level earnings of the baby boomers—lower, more unequal, and less steady than those of more experienced workers—have distorted the trends in measured income patterns. If these workers are on the lower end of the same seniority and age-based wage track as older workers, then aggregate trends toward declining incomes and greater inequality will be reversed as they grow older.

There is no doubt that the age shift of the labor force has affected living standards and inequality, but the youthfulness of the labor force does not explain the trends. For example, the spiralling unemployment of recent years cannot be attributed primarily to an increase in the number of young workers, or in new entrants to the labor force. Labor economist Michael Podgursky concluded that while the greater number of young workers pushed up the unemployment rate after 1969, this effect has since declined. Between 1975 and 1982, over half of the increase in the unemployment rate was accounted for by prime-age men (25-54); prime-age women accounted for about one-fourth.[17]

Furthermore, greater income inequality is not just a baby boom phenomenon. Poverty economists Peter Gottschalk and Michael Dooley found that inequality in earnings has been rising within all age groups of working men, even after controlling for the level of education, experience, and unemployment.[18] Income trends can be better explained by examining the interaction of structural changes in the family, economy, and government.

• Family Revolution

The major demographic backdrop for the trend toward increasing inequality is the increase in non-nuclear, non-male-headed families. In 1955, 9.0 percent of white families and 20.7 percent of families of color were headed by women. By 1985, 12.8 percent of white families and 43.7 percent of black families were comprised of women and their dependents.[19]

Historically, poverty rates for female-headed families have been high. The disproportionate risk of poverty among female-headed families stems from four enduring structural characteristics of the economy and of families. First, while far more jobs are available to women now than in the past, the likelihood of employment (particularly full-time employment) is still lower for women than men. Second, while there has been a slight improvement in the ratio of white female to white male wages, and substantial improvement in the female-male wage ratio for blacks, women's wages remain considerably lower than men's. Third, single and divorced mothers continue to shoulder the primary responsibility for their children, stretching the ability of

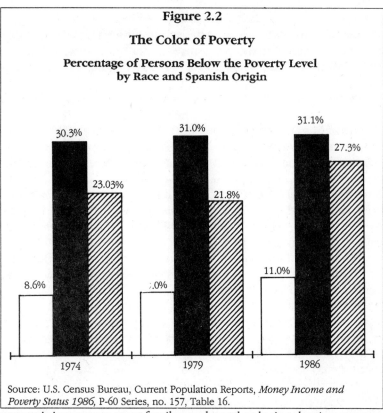

Figure 2.2

The Color of Poverty

**Percentage of Persons Below the Poverty Level
by Race and Spanish Origin**

Source: U.S. Census Bureau, Current Population Reports, *Money Income and
Poverty Status 1986,* P-60 Series, no. 157, Table 16.

women's incomes to meet family needs, and reducing the time women
have available to work for pay. Finally, female-headed families are disproportionately black or Latino, and face not only sexual but also racial discrimination. Many poor black female-headed families would also
be poor if the head were male. A recent study showed that 55 percent
of the difference between black and white poverty rates comes from
higher poverty rates for blacks of all household types, not from the
greater prevalence of female-headed families.[20]

It is possible to argue that new economic opportunities have
reduced many women's economic dependence on men, diminished
their need to marry as a way to claim part of a husband's income, and
caused the "feminization of poverty."[21] Particularly for middle-class married women of all races, the availability of clerical and service jobs could
tide them over, for example, in the approximately five years between
divorce and remarriage. Even though they might experience a temporary spell of poverty, they still were in better economic shape than
their mothers would have been in similar circumstances. Thus even the

growth of low-wage job opportunities for women enabled many women to leave or postpone marriage. The recent increase in the number of poor women who are not married is due in important measure simply to the increasing numbers of single women, rather than to an increase in the prevalence of poverty among this group.

Poverty was "feminized," in short, not because of an increasing rate of poverty *among* unmarried women, but largely because the poverty rates of male-headed families fell faster than those of female-headed families, and because the *number* of unmarried women increased. As traditions fade, the family is increasingly doing without its principal source of funds—men. And the government has not made up much of the difference.

• Economic Dislocation

The American dream—an upwardly mobile married couple with a comfortable home and new car—is fading. Its demise is due at least as much to structural economic changes as it is to the erosion of the nuclear family. The final tally is not in, but a growing body of evidence suggests that opportunities for secure, well-paid, full-time employment are shrinking.

The real wage (i.e. adjusted for inflation) of the American worker is falling. Between 1973 and 1979, the average real wage of non-agricultural production workers in the private sector fell by 4.3 percent. Between 1979 and 1986, real wages fell even more—by 5.9 percent.[22] Whatever the economic benefits of the Reagan-Volcker assault on inflation, they have not yet shown up in real wage gains.

Structural unemployment is also on the rise. Using data collected by Dun and Bradstreet, economists Barry Bluestone and Bennett Harrison found that "runaway shops, shutdowns, and permanent physical cutbacks may have cost the country as many as 38 million jobs."[23] (The number of jobs lost to cutbacks short of closure is difficult to determine. According to Bluestone and Harrison, more than 32 million jobs were lost as a direct result of plant, store, and office shutdowns, plus runaway shops.) Economist Candee Harris found that, due to plant closures alone, an average of 800,000 jobs were lost annually from 1978-1982 in manufacturing facilities with 100 or more employees.[24]

This dislocation of workers has continued under the Reagan administration. There were 5.1 million displaced workers in January 1984—workers with at least three years of experience—who had lost their jobs between 1979 and 1983 because of plant closings, relocations, slack work, or the cancellation of positions or shifts.[25]

Among these displaced workers, the median duration of unemployment was six months.[26] About one-third had not received any unemployment compensation; one-half of those who did had exhausted their benefits by 1984. At least one-half of those re-employed were earning less than they had in their old jobs.[27]

Estimates of long-term earnings losses among permanently displaced prime-age men vary by industry. In 1978, former auto, steel, meatpacking, aerospace, and flat glass workers had lost one-sixth of their income six years after the initial job loss.[28] A 1985 study of displaced steelworkers found that 61 percent of laid-off production workers who found new jobs were re-employed as laborers or in service sector industries.[29] The loss in income was apparent in changes in the former steelworkers' educational plans for their children: 21 percent had to withdraw or were unable to enroll their children in college.[30]

The job problem goes beyond the absolute lack of employment opportunity. The structure of jobs also appears to be heavily implicated in the growth of inequality. One study found that between 1958 and 1977, the distribution of wage income among men with some earnings became more unequal.[31] Another study concluded that the inequality of male earnings grew by 2 percent annually over this period.[32] For women, inequality changed little during this time, but because of greater differences among women in the number of hours worked for pay, inequality among women was greater than among men.[33]

The service industries, highly unequal in terms of workers' pay, are the fastest growing in the United States. This sector (including trade, finance, insurance, real estate, and government) accounted for 56.7 percent of total U.S. employment in 1940. By 1960, the figure had jumped to 62.3 percent and then to 71.5 percent in 1980. In contrast, goods-producing employment (including mining, manufacturing, and construction) shrank from 43.3 percent in 1940 to 37.7 percent in 1960 to 28.5 percent in 1980.[34]

The shift from manufacturing to service industries is the result of long-term social and economic trends. Visible in nearly all advanced industrialized countries, the shift reflects increased affluence; as people get richer, they tend to spend more on services.[35] As more women have entered the paid labor force, market demand for services formerly provided inside the home has skyrocketed.

The structural shift also reflects the long-term decline in the international competitiveness of U.S. manufacturing. The U.S. share of world trade in manufactured goods dropped steadily from 25 percent in 1953 to 15.6 percent in 1979.[36] While deterioration in the U.S. trade position predates conservative economics, the high value of the dollar generated by the Volcker-Reagan strategy decimated U.S. exports, driving many workers out of manufacturing and into service sector jobs in the early 1980s. Despite the subsequent fall of the price of the dollar abroad, U.S. exports have not substantially increased and the manufacturing sector has not expanded to make up for the drastic loss of jobs.

• Government Retrenchment

Trends toward larger numbers of female-headed households, lower pay, higher unemployment, and greater earnings inequality were well established before the onset of economic orthodoxy in the late 1970s. These trends, however, were substantially blunted by the structure of taxes and transfers during the 1970s.[37]

Transfers also maintained a ceiling in the 1970s on the rising levels of poverty which were being produced by the changing structure of the economy and the family. In 1970, the fraction of people whose incomes would be classified as poor in the absence of government transfers began to rise. From 1969 to 1974, the so-called pre-transfer poverty rate rose. However, total cash and in-kind government transfers per household rose as well. As a result, the post-transfer poverty rate fell by over 10 percent (see Figure 2.3).[38]

The same structural trends in the economy and the family persisted into the early 1980s. But under the reign of conservative economics, the government exacerbated rather than softened their impact. Federal policy changes after the Reagan-Volcker initiative apparently lowered average disposable income from what it would have been otherwise.

Researchers Marilyn Moon and Isabel Sawhill at the Urban Institute compared the outcome of trickle-down economic policy with simulated outcomes of likely alternatives.[39] Their benchmark alternative policy scenario was not a liberal wish-list—it included a continuing high level of unemployment, for example, and policies which would reduce the relative incomes of the poor. It did however, incorporate less military spending, greater domestic spending, fewer tax cuts, and a more expansive monetary policy than the policies of the Reagan administration. The simulation indicated that real disposable family income would have increased by 4 percent, compared to an actual increase of 3.5 percent. They concluded that the Reagan-Volcker policies had reduced incomes by 0.5 percent (see Figure 2.4).

The disappointing growth of average incomes is the good news. The bad news is that the free-market experiment contributed dramatically to widening income gaps. Under Reagan-Volcker policies, the rich got substantially richer and the poor much poorer, even in addition to

Figure 2.3

Retreat from the War on Poverty

Poverty Rates with and without Government Transfers, 1965-1985
percent reduction in poverty

Year	pre-transfer incidence	official (post-transfer) incidence	incidence due to transfers
1965	21.3	17.3	4.0
1966	—	15.7	—
1967	19.4	14.3	5.1
1968	18.2	12.8	5.4
1969	17.7	12.1	5.6
1970	18.8	12.6	6.2
1971	19.6	12.5	7.1
1972	19.2	11.9	7.3
1973	19.0	11.1	7.9
1974	20.3	11.2	9.1
1975	22.0	12.3	9.7
1976	21.0	11.8	9.2
1977	21.0	11.6	9.4
1978	20.2	11.4	8.8
1979	20.5	11.7	8.8
1980	21.9	13.0	8.9
1981	23.1	14.0	9.1
1982	24.0	15.0	9.0
1983	24.2	15.3	8.9
1984	22.9	14.4	8.5
1985	22.4	14.0	8.4

Source: For 1965-1983, Sheldon Danziger and Peter Gottschalk, "The Poverty of Losing Ground," *Challenge*, May-June 1985, p. 34. For 1984 and 1985, Sheldon Danziger, Robert Haveman, and Robert Plotnick, "Antipoverty Policy: Effects on the Poor and Nonpoor," in *Fighting Poverty: What Works and What Doesn't*, Sheldon Danziger and Daniel Weinberg, eds., Cambridge: Harvard University Press, 1986, p. 54.

the increasing inequality the market was producing on its own. Moon and Sawhill concluded that the poorest 20 percent of U.S. families would have lost 3.5 percent of their 1980 income under the hypothetical alternative policy; the next poorest 20 percent would have gained only 1.3 percent. Under the Reagan-Volcker policies, both groups were net losers: the bottom 20 percent in reality lost 7.6 percent, while the next poorest 20 percent lost 1.7 percent. Only the very top 20 percent of all families were net gainers under the first Reagan administration. Their incomes would have increased by 7.1 percent anyway—but the Reagan-Volcker program gave them even more. Their actual incomes increased 8.7 percent.

Figure 2.4

Conservative Economics Fuel Poverty

**Contributions of Reagan Policies to Changes in the Level
and Distribution of Real Disposable Family Income, 1980-1984
(in 1982 dollars)**

income quintiles

	bottom	second	third	fourth	fifth	total
percentage change since 1980	-7.6	-1.7	0.9	3.4	8.7	3.5
percentage change since 1980 under alternative policy scenario	-3.5	1.3	2.6	4.0	7.1	4.0
difference attributable to Reagan policies	-4.1	-3.0	-1.7	-0.6	1.6	-0.5

Source: Marilyn Moon and Isabel Sawhill, "Family Incomes: Gainers and Losers," in John L. Palmer and Isabel V. Sawhill, eds., *The Reagan Record, An Assessment of America's Domestic Frontier,* Urban Institute, Washington D.C., p. 329.

Married-couple families experienced small increases in disposable incomes over these years, although the simulation indicated that Reagan-Volcker policies reduced these gains from what they otherwise would have been, particularly for one-earner families. Female-headed and black families bore the brunt of the losses. Black families would have gained 0.5 percent on average under the alternative policy scenario, but the policy changes left them with a 2.1 percent decline. Female-headed families, which would have otherwise experienced a 0.5 percent loss, contended with 3.3 percent less disposable income in 1984 than in 1980.

• Can We Do Better?

The explicit logic behind supply-side economics—and some corporate reindustrialization schemes as well—is that slow growth or actual reductions in the standard of living are necessary in the short run to reignite the engine of economic growth. Advocates argue that while equality may be a morally desirable goal, it has conflicted directly with efficiency, and thus with the country's ability to improve the livelihood of its people. Inequality is considered unfortunate but necessary to motivate work effort, innovation, risk-taking, and saving, all of which make an economy grow. Hard workers, innovators, risk-takers, and

savers must get more than others to insure their continuing contribution to growth. Free-market economics further contends that any institution which meddles with the market mechanism, especially
government, impairs the economy's ability to eliminate poverty and en-
hance general well-being in the long run.

In spite of the rhetoric, the free-market experiment left the bottom 80 percent of the population significantly worse off. Researchers
at the Wisconsin Institute for Research on Poverty concluded that even
with an improbable decade of sustained annual growth with no reces-
sions, no further program cuts, and a miraculous halt in long established trends toward inequality, it would still take over a decade to
reduce the poverty rate to its 1979 level.[40] The vast majority of people
are no better off than they were in 1979. Barring a change in economic
policy, they are likely to be worse off and deeply divided in the years
to come. Conservative economics, with carrots for the rich and sticks
for the rest, simply has not trickled the benefits down to those who
need them most.

CHAPTER 3

Reaganomics and Racial Inequality

In 1963, Martin Luther King's dream of a multiracial society of free and equal citizens electrified millions of Americans. In the decade which followed, black Americans and other people of color made significant political and economic progress.[1] But on the eve of the twenty-fifth anniversary of King's catalyzing vision, the United States is moving not nearer but further from making his dream a reality.

Economic, social, and political reversals for people of color began in the late 1970s. They are the result of trends that predate the Reagan era, particularly the dissolution of the civil rights movement, the end of the postwar economic expansion, and the persistence of racist ideologies.

But conservative economic strategies—including an assault on the public sector and the use of unemployment to discipline labor—have dramatically accelerated the economic decline of people of color. Furthermore, conservative rhetoric has heightened a dog-eat-dog ideology which holds that people of color can advance only at the expense of whites. As Rosalyn Carter put it, the conservative reign has made white America comfortable with its prejudices.

In short, while progress toward racial equality slowed before 1981, the Reagan administration has played a critical role in worsening the economic position of people of color. As a result, race relations have deteriorated and the United States is becoming a nation ever more deeply divided.

• The New Age of Reaction

From the mid-1960s to the mid-1970s, people of color made significant economic gains relative to whites. Since the late 1970s, however, and especially since the advent of the Reagan administration, the trend toward economic gains for people of color has been reversed. Indeed, the Reagan administration has attempted to dismantle the institutional structure put into place in the 1960s and 1970s to combat racial and economic discrimination.

The current period of racist reaction parallels an earlier period of American history marked by growing racial division. After 1877, reaction set in against the major political and economic advances blacks had made in the decade and a half following emancipation. Termed the Black Reconstruction by historian W.E.B. DuBois, blacks made significant gains in land ownership, voting rights, and political power during these fifteen years. The reaction reversed most of these gains, triggering policies which disenfranchised black voters, increased violence against blacks, and intensified the economic exploitation of black workers.

Commentators on the current scene, such as economist Michael Reich of the University of California at Berkeley, have warned of a repetition of this tragic pattern. Noting the gains in employment and occupational mobility achieved between the end of World War II and the mid-1970s, he observes:

> In the 1980s, many of these indices show signs of worsening. And under Reagan, the political direction of the federal government on racial matters is once again reversing. The second Reconstruction has clearly ended and we are already well into a second Era of Reaction.[2]

The reaction goes far beyond the economy and touches virtually all aspects of our society.

- The racial composition of the judicial system, which had progressed toward parity during the late 1970s, turned toward racial exclusion in the 1980s. Twenty-one percent of Jimmy Carter's appointments to District Courts were black, Latino, or Asian; only 7 percent of Ronald Reagan's first term appointments were people of color[3];
- The proportion of black students entering medical school declined over the past decade, despite the fact that black applications to medical schools increased and black applicants' test scores improved more rapidly than those of whites. According to a recent study, the acceptance rate for black applicants fell from 43 percent to 40 percent between 1974 and 1983, while the acceptance rate for whites rose from 35 percent to 50 percent. The study's co-author, Dr. Steven Shea of Columbia University's College of Physicians and Surgeons, concluded: "I think there's been a general shift in the social climate, and the importance of achieving equality for minorities has diminished on the national agenda"[4];

- According to linguists, white and black English are becoming increasingly dissimilar. University of Pennsylvania Professor William Labov, author of a 1985 study of "black English vernacular," concludes that ordinary communication between whites and blacks is becoming increasingly difficult. According to Labov, the divergence of language reflects increasing racial segregation and social isolation[5];
- Fewer blacks and Latinos are enrolling in colleges. Between 1976 and 1983, the percentage of black high school graduates enrolling in college declined from 33.5 percent to 27 percent. The Latino percentage went down from 35.8 percent to 31.4 percent. For whites, the figure remained unchanged at 33 percent.[6]

Less easily measured has been the amplification of ideologies of white supremacy. These racist ideologies often build on such touchstones of conservative economic rhetoric as the belief in the biological determination of economic success and the closely associated notion that in a market society, those who are less successful have only their own moral or genetic inferiority to blame.

The Reagan administration, in short, has not only attempted to restore an economic order reminiscent of the days of Harding and Coolidge; it has also helped to reconstruct and consolidate a *racial* order which had been challenged by the social movements and economic trends of the 1960s and early 1970s. Much of the new Age of Reaction has been catalyzed by economic and social policies whose effects, if not intent, can only be called racist.

• The Reversal of a Decade of Economic Gains for People of Color

Political pressure and economic trends in the 1950s and 1960s improved the relative living standards of people of color. The median income of families of color jumped from 52 percent to 63 percent of the white level between 1959 and 1969. Women of color made especially rapid income gains. Unemployment among all people of color dipped from 2 to 1.8 times that of whites.

During the 1970s, many economists and others heralded the imminent end of racial discrimination. They claimed that economic gains by people of color were the result of long-term historical trends, built into the very structure of liberal capitalist America. The *Economic Report of the President, 1974,* signed by Richard Nixon, hailed the "long run narrowing of the racial income difference." The *Report* attributed the gains to the joint effects of growing racial tolerance and a capitalist economic system in which competition forces cost-conscious busi-

Figure 3.1

A Reversal of Gains

Postwar Trends in the Economic Status of People of Color*

	1953	1956	1959	1969	1973	1979	1986
ratio of black to white median income							
men	.59	.56	.58	.67	.69	.62	.63
women	.49	.45	.53	.79	.90	.91	.85
families	.56	.53	.52	.63	.58	.57	.57
unemployment rates							
white men	2.5	3.4	4.6	2.5	3.8	4.5	6.0
white women	3.1	4.2	5.3	4.2	5.3	5.9	6.1
black men	4.8	7.9	11.5	5.3	8.0	11.4	14.8
black women	4.1	9.0	9.4	7.8	11.1	13.3	14.2
labor force participation rates							
white men	86.1	85.6	83.8	80.2	79.5	78.6	76.9
white women	33.4	35.7	36.0	41.8	44.1	50.5	55.0
black men	86.2	85.1	83.4	76.9	73.4	71.3	71.2
black women	43.6	47.3	47.7	49.8	49.3	53.1	56.9

* Data from 1963 to 1969 refer to "blacks and others." Data from 1973 to 1986 refer to blacks only. Years represent peaks of postwar business cycles.

Sources: U.S. Census Bureau, *Money Income of Households Families, and Persons in the United States*, P-60 Series, various years; U.S. Bureau of Labor Statistics, *Handbook of Labor Statistics*, July 1985; and U.S. Bureau of Labor Statistics, *Employment and Earnings*, January 1987.

nesses to hire the most qualified and productive workers at the lowest price—regardless of race.[7]

Trends since the early 1970s do not support this assessment, however, and cast doubt on the positive role played by the capitalist system in promoting racial equality and harmony. Figure 3.1 surveys key indicators of the economic status of black families and individuals in the United States; the data correspond to peak years in the business cycle. The ratio of black to white individual median income was relatively constant during the first three business cycles of the postwar period, but increased sharply during the long expansion of the 1960s. Between 1959 and 1969, black men increased their median income by 9 percentage points relative to white men. Over the next cycle, from 1969 to 1973, black men's median income improved slightly relative to white men's. Most of these gains were lost by 1979, after the 1974 recession. Paradoxically, it appears that between 1979 and 1986 black men did not lose ground relative to white men.

A closer look reveals a different story. During the Reagan years, median weekly earnings for black men working full-time declined from 76 percent of white men's in 1979 to 73 percent in 1986 (see Figure

3.2). The loss in relative earnings was most pronounced for workers under age twenty-four.

Black women followed a similar income pattern relative to white women but were able to make more significant gains. Between 1959 and 1969, black women improved their income relative to white women by 25 percentage points (see Figure 3.1). The following business cycle brought another large increase in the ratio between black and white women's median incomes from .79 to .90. In the late 1970s, gains slowed to a virtual halt, and the Reagan years have brought on a sharp reversal of gains.

Despite the gains in median income for both black men and women relative to whites since the 1960s, overall family income ratios have barely budged since the Civil Rights Act became law. In part, gains for black households have been offset by the rapid increase in white women's labor force participation and with it the increase in white family income. Black women's labor force participation has increased but not as rapidly as white women's labor force participation while black men's labor force participation rate has fallen more quickly than that of white men (see Figure 3.1).

Pennsylvania State University economist Peter Bohmer attempted to discern whether racial economic progress had actually stopped or if the statistics merely reflected changes in the business cycle, especially the severe recession of the early 1980s. In a detailed statistical study, he found there was no improvement in the relative earnings of men of color to white men in the private sector since 1975. This followed a strong upward trend in earlier years. Similar results were obtained for women workers.[8]

Figure 3.2

A Closer Look at the Reagan Era

Ratio of Median Weekly Earnings of Full-Time Workers by Age, Sex, Race, and Hispanic Origin, 1979 and 1986

	1979				1986		
		16-24	24 +	Total		16-24	24+	Total
black/white								
men	.76	.83	.75		.73	.84	.72
women	.93	.92	.92		.89	.90	.88
Hispanic/white								
men	.73	.88	.74		.69	.85	.68
women	.83	.90	.84		.81	.92	.81

Source: U.S. Department of Labor, Bureau of Labor Statistics, *Employment and Earnings,* January 1987.

• Does the Market Promote Racial Equality?

The improvements before 1975 should not have prompted the congratulatory attitude adopted in Nixon's *Economic Report of the President*, for they stemmed not from market forces but from two quite particular and time-bound events. First was black migration out of the agricultural South and into the industrial North during the 1950s and 1960s. Migration was responsible for most of the gains in black male income relative to white male income and changed the nature of male employment dramatically. In 1950, nearly 25 percent of employed black men held jobs in agriculture. Another 25 percent were employed as laborers. By 1970, less than 4 percent worked in agriculture and only 16 percent were laborers. Instead, black men moved into jobs primarily as operators and craft and clerical workers in the higher-paying industrial sector.[9]

While the migration boosted black male income, the relative position of black men worsened in the Northeast. Indeed, in both the Northeast and Midwest, the ratio of the median income of "non-whites" relative to white men has gotten worse since 1953.[10] In 1953, it was .75 in both the Northeast and Midwest. By 1985, the ratio had decreased to .67 in the Northeast and .65 in the Midwest.[11]

The second factor raising the economic standing of people of color relative to whites was a changing occupational structure for women of color. Black women were drawn from work in private households to jobs in the service sector, especially government employ-

credit: Bob Englehart for the Hartford Courant

ment or clerical work. Over 42 percent of employed black women worked in private households in 1950. By 1980, the figure had fallen to 5 percent.[12] Better jobs have translated into higher relative incomes for black women. While all women continue to earn substantially less than men, the improvement for "non-white" women helped to narrow the earnings gap between whites and people of color.

In short, improvements in the relative incomes of people of color were not spurred by the unhampered workings of the labor market but by migration, job opportunities outside of domestic work for women of color, and public sector expansion. Perhaps more important, the data on relative incomes mask what can only be called an ongoing disaster on the jobs front. People of color have suffered disproportionately high and growing rates of unemployment.

Since the mid-1970s, the employment picture for both whites and people of color has worsened considerably. Unemployment has been consistently higher than at any time during the entire postwar period and it has been disproportionately higher for black men and black women. In the second quarter of 1985, barely one half of all black families had a member working full-time; of the remainder, well over one-quarter had no member working for pay at all.[13] The situation was slightly better for Hispanic families; two out of three families had at least one full-time employee.

Since the late 1970s, the gap has grown between overall black and white unemployment. Between 1959 and 1974, black male unemployment was 2.2 times that of whites; between 1976 and 1984, it grew to 2.4 times that of whites. The absolute spread between the two rates swelled from 5.1 percentage points to 8.8 percentage points. For women, the corresponding unemployment ratio rose from 1.93 to 2.18 and the gap between the rates rose from 5 to 8.2 percentage points.[14]

• Reconstructing the Racial Order

Progress toward racial economic equality sputtered in the late 1970s. Since 1979, however, three particular aspects of federal government policy have intensified the attack on the economic status of people of color: macroeconomic policies, spending priorities and tax reform, and civil rights policy.

The "last hired, first fired" status of people of color in labor markets means that generally high levels of unemployment hurt people of color disproportionately. One Bureau of Labor Statistics study found that, while both black and white workers were thrown out of work during contractions in the postwar period, unemployment grew faster for black than for white workers during the contraction. Black workers

were disproportionately hurt during periods of slow economic activity. Conversely, when workers returned to their jobs during expansions, unemployment rates for blacks, although higher in absolute terms, went down at faster rates.[15]

While all workers are subjected to the discipline of unemployment in the capitalist economy, the unequal impact of the business cycle upon people of color makes them a "buffer" against the full effect of the cycle upon other segments of workers. The ability of the Reagan administration to gain political support for a macroeconomic policy of high unemployment may be connected to the fact that the costs of unemployment and under-employment are heavily concentrated among people of color.

The second prong of the *de facto* assault on the economic status of people of color is the shift in spending priorities from social programs to military procurement. The first phase of cuts in federal social programs, initiated in Reagan's first term in office, have hit people of color especially hard. According to recent studies, the average black family lost three times as much in income and benefits as did the average white family in 1981. The average Latino family lost twice as much.[16]

Ten major programs have suffered the largest budget cuts (see Figure 3.3). Most of these programs directly or indirectly subsidize poverty rates for the working poor. Poverty rates for people of color who work are substantially higher than for other sectors of the population. The largest cuts have been for programs, like CETA (which was eliminated completely), which directly affect the functioning of the labor market and the training available for the working poor. While the administration's rhetoric proclaims that the alternative to welfare must

be employment, the programs which support this alternative have been all but wiped out in the reorganization of the budget.

The first term of the Reagan administration reorganized not only government expenditures but the tax structure as well. The 1981 tax act offered tax-cutting tailored to the affluent taxpayer. The "supply-side" reform package ended a tradition of regular revisions to the tax code which benefited low-income families. The net result of changes in federal tax policies—standard deductions, personal exemptions, and earned income tax credit—has been a shift in the tax burden to middle- and low-income groups.

Since blacks and Latinos are heavily over-represented in low- and moderate-income groups (given their limited access to business ownership and financial assets), tax reform aimed at affluent taxpayers benefits them very little. The Congressional Budget Office projected that households with incomes under $20,000 per year would lose $19.7 billion between 1983 and 1985. Conversely, households with incomes above $80,000 per year would gain $34.9 billion. Sixty percent of Latino families and 63 percent of black families are in the under-$20,000 income category. On a per capita basis, this redistribution of income represents an average loss of $1,100 for families below $10,000 and a gain of $24,000 for families over $80,000. Income losses per household in 1982 due to tax changes averaged $575 for Latino and $457 for blacks.[17]

Despite the voracity of social cuts, increases in military spending and the 1981 tax cuts have increased the annual deficit. In response to the "spend and borrow" debacle, Congress passed the Balanced Budget and Emergency Control Act of 1985, popularly known as the Gramm-Rudman-Hollings Act, GRH for short. The GRH represents the second wave of cuts—now required by law—in many of the already decimated

Figure 3.3

Budget Cuts' Impact on People of Color

Size of Budget Cuts in Programs With High Black and Latino Participation

Program	dimensions of cuts for FY1985	% of participants who are:		
		black	Latino	black & Latino
CETA	100.0	30.3	14.7	45.0
employment training	38.6	37.3	11.9	49.2
work incentive	35.1	33.6	17.2	50.8
child nutrition	28.0	17.4	9.9	27.3
legal services	28.0	24.4	13.5	37.9
compensatory education	19.5	31.5	13.5	13.5
Pell grants, for higher education	15.6	34.0	—	—
Food Stamps	13.8	36.8	10.5	47.3
AFDC	14.3	45.7	13.5	59.2
subsidized housing	11.4	45.3	10.8	56.1

Source: John L. Palmer and Isabel V. Sawhill, eds., *The Reagan Record: An Assessment of America's Changing Domestic Priorities*, Urban Institute, August 1984, based on data from the Office of Management and Budget.

domestic programs with high levels of participation by people of color. Among the exempt budget items are social security benefits, interest on the federal debt, prior year obligations, and some programs targeting the poor such as AFDC, Food Stamps, and Medicaid. A second category includes civil and military retirement, Special Milk programs, and others which have been indexed to inflation and frozen at their 1985 expenditures levels. Half the cuts are expected to come from this category by reducing automatic cost-of-living increases. In a third category—Health Services (e.g. Medicare)—budget cuts range from 1-2 percent, but the real impact is likely to be much greater depending on increasing costs in the health industry. All other budget line items, are subject to across the board reductions.[18]

The structure of the GRH budget cuts is important considering the significant change in the distribution of federal spending between 1978 and 1986. One way to measure the relative size of programs is to compare them to their percentage of the total output produced (referred to as the Gross National Product or GNP). During this period the share of social security benefits and net interest payments (both exempt programs under GRH) increased by 0.5 and 1.7 percent of GNP respectively, and the share of Medicare expenditures increased 0.7 percent of GNP. With these big-ticket items totally excluded, or protected by a 2 percent cap as is Medicare, GRH will impose reductions on defense and all other domestic programs.[19]

A study conducted by the National Urban League concluded:

> The distributive effects of GRH are essentially negative. Beginning with a budgetary base already insufficient for most human needs, including priority concerns for blacks identified in the Congressional Black Caucus Alternative Budget....When increases in the needs of the black community resulting both from absolute population increases and increasingly needy populations are combined with increases in the cost of goods and services paid by diminishing federal dollars, the actual GRH reductions range from 8.6 percent to 11 percent of the 1985 base budget.[20]

Additionally, the Tax Reform Act (TRA) of 1986 will reinforce the regressive tendency of the 1981 tax reform. While the increase in the "no-tax status" (i.e. the minimum income before being required to pay federal income taxes) should take some low-income households off the income tax rolls, the TRA also lowered the marginal tax rates on the highest end of the income scale by almost one-half.[21] In 1980, the marginal personal income tax rate for a family of four with half the median income was 18 and for the median and twice the median income families was 24 and 43, respectively (see Figure 3.4). By 1986, the rate was 4 percentage points lower for families with half the median income and 2 and 5 percentage points lower for median and twice-median income families respectively. The 1981 tax reform lowered rates across the board, but high-income families benefitted the most. The

---

Figure 3.4

Tax Reform?

Marginal Personal Income Tax Rates for Four-Person Families Before and After the Tax Reform Act of 1986

Year	tax rates for family of four		
	earning half median income	earning median income	earning twice median income
1965	14	17	22
1980	18	24	43
1986	14	22	38
1988 (with TRA)	15	15	28
	change in marginal tax rates		
1965-1980	+4	+7	+21
1980-1986	-4	-2	- 5
1986-1988	+1	-7	-10
1980-1988	-3	-9	-15

Source: *Economic Report of the President, 1987,* p. 80.

TRA of 1986 will increase the tax burden for families with half the median income to the same burden as those with the median income and actually decrease by over 25 percent the tax burden on families with twice the median income over their 1986 levels.[22]

The reorganization of the budget toward defense and away from social needs will also alter the structure of employment and the position of people of color in the labor market. Defense spending is projected to rise from 5.2 percent of GNP and 22.7 percent of the budget in 1980 to 7.5 percent of GNP and 36 percent of the total federal budget by 1990.[23] Although the overall effect of military spending on employment is controversial, there is less doubt about its employment effect upon people of color.[24]

Most of the increase in military spending under Reagan is concentrated in capital-intensive industries largely closed to people of color—weapons procurement, research and development, military construction. This spending will grow from 37.3 percent of each defense dollar in 1980 to 50 percent in 1986.[25] The shift in U.S. government spending priorities from human services to military procurement has decreased job opportunities for people of color. Blacks and other people of color, as well as white women, are significantly under-represented in the major military procurement industries. Using 1980 employment data, a hypothetical shift of a million jobs from health services, educational services, and social services to aerospace, communications, and electronics (prime military industries) would generate a net loss of 320,000 jobs for white women and 66,000 jobs for black women. By contrast, white men would gain 386,000 jobs. The job losses of black men, who have more employment in the military-related industries, would be almost completely offset by job gains.[26]

Equally important is that government employment has slowed and levelled off. Because the government at all levels employs disproportionately greater numbers of people of color than the private sector, the recent shift in jobs from the public to the private sector of the economy has tended to reduce employment opportunities for people of color. Bohmer calculated the impact of this slowdown of public sector growth on total employment for black workers. He concludes:

> If government employment had continued to grow at its 1962-1976 annual rate...and employed blacks and whites at the 1984 composition of the government [employment], 247,000 more black men and half a million more black women would have had jobs in 1984. ...[T]he continued growth in public sector employment

would have eliminated about half of the growth in the unemployment gap for men and the entire growth of the gap for women.[27]

• The Assault on Affirmative Action

One of the most important accomplishments of the civil rights movement was the legal promise of equal employment opportunity and affirmative action policies. The impact of affirmative action on the employment of people of color, particularly black males, was generally positive. Affirmative action encouraged the demand for black males in white collar and craft occupations, particularly in large and expanding corporations. Blacks found better paying jobs and the demand for low-skilled blacks increased as others moved up the occupation ladder.[28] The Reagan administration's position on discrimination in employment and affirmative action should be understood as part of its general hostility to civil rights. The record is clear: proposed tax exemptions for segregated schools, judicial harassment of voting rights activists in the South, exclusion from judiciary and executive appointments, assault on the U.S. Civil Rights Commission.

The Reagan administration has opposed affirmative action on the grounds of "reverse discrimination," the idea that using affirmative action goals and quotas to eliminate racial discrimination creates new forms of discrimination against whites and results in less efficient production. According to this view, racial oppression is something that existed in the past and our generation should not be forced to pay for our ancestors' mistakes. Contrary to the administration's belief, there is no evidence supporting a decline of workers' productivity due to changes in racial composition (as would be the case if less qualified, but white, workers were hired), nor that white workers have been adversely affected by affirmative action. In most cases, the cost to firms and losses to whites of affirmative action are very small.[29]

In addition to its attack on the government front, the administration has altered the very definition of racial discrimination, seeking to disallow the use of simple statistical evidence of discriminatory hiring patterns. Rather than evaluating claims of racial discrimination based on hiring *outcomes*, the Reagan administration has argued that *intent* to discriminate must be proven. In upholding the Nixon administration's use of such evidence, the U.S. Court of Appeals for the Ninth District in California wrote in 1985:

> Since the passage of the Civil Rights Act of 1964, the courts have frequently relied upon statistical evidence to prove a violation. In many cases the only available avenue of proof is the use of racial

statistics to uncover clandestine and covert discrimination by the employer or union involved. [30]

The Reagan era is coming to an abrupt end. The administration that promised to balance the budget, make American products more competitive in international markets, and raise the standard of living for average Americans has generated the largest budget and trade deficits in American history, and the average family is worse off today than it was in 1980. People of color, however, have paid an even higher price for the conservative economic experiment.

credit: Nick Thorkelson

• The Politics of Race

During the 1980s, people of color received economic and social blows, the effects of which will last for decades to come. In the 1960s, the civil rights movement demanded changes that undermined a centuries-old system of racial oppression. Perhaps unwittingly, the conservative logic of high levels of unemployment, a military buildup, social program cuts, and dogmatic faith in the market is well on the way to reconstructing an old social order where white people benefit at the expense of people of color. Racial policies, explicit or implicit in the intricacies of national economic policies, are an important element in the emerging realignment of social and economic forces in American society.

Can a new civil rights movement be rekindled to counter this assault? Much depends on coming to terms with the thorny question of who benefits from racial discrimination. Mobilizing a mass movement against racism in the United States will involve confronting the perceived interests of some whites in perpetuating the racial order.

Employers, for example, can turn racism into higher profits in two ways: directly, when they pay less-than-average wages to people of color; and indirectly, when they are able to keep a divided labor force in a weak bargaining position. In 1980, employers' direct gain from wage discrimination—the extra amount they would have had to pay if black workers earned the same as whites—reached $25 billion, a substantial fraction of corporate profits.[31]

But these were only the direct profits. A more accurate estimate would also include additional profits from lower wages paid to white workers because of a divided labor force. This amount is equivalent to the income lost by white workers because of racial discrimination. Indeed, there is a strong inverse relationship in local U.S. labor markets between the relative income standing of people of color and the real income of white workers: where the income gap between whites and people of color is particularly wide, the average income of white workers is lower than where the gap is narrower.[32] In short, white workers as a whole are impoverished, not enriched, by racial discrimination.

Nonetheless, white workers do benefit from racism. If there is a certain amount of unemployment to be "shared" by workers and a given number of good jobs to go around, white workers benefit from relatively lower unemployment, better access to good jobs, and higher income relative to workers who face discrimination.

The issue of white workers' gains or losses from racism in labor markets is controversial. To any given white worker—individually unable to alter the distribution of income between capital and labor or the availability of well-paying safe jobs—racial preference for whites in hiring increases the chances of economic and personal well-being and security. This worker will likely see the economy as a zero-sum game in which any other worker's gains reduce his or her opportunities. In a society rampant with racial prejudice, it is not surprising that many whites focus their anger on people of color. But for workers and communities as a whole, being divided from within is clearly not advantageous. The long history of U.S. labor movement struggles for higher wages, better working conditions, and greater say in the political and economic process reveals that inter-racial and inter-ethnic unity has typically been the key to success, and its absence, the assurance of failure.

Demographic trends may favor an increase in the political power of people of color. Because of an emphasis on voter registration, the economic reverses of the past decade have not been mirrored in the electoral sphere and it also likely that electoral successes by black and Latino political candidates will continue. According to estimates by political scientist Kenneth Dolbeare, people of color will comprise over a quarter of the population in such pivotal electoral states as Texas, New York, Florida, and Illinois before the end of the century. In California, they will form half.[33] In at least ten other states, people of color will comprise at least a quarter of the population. Political strategies will ignore the swing potential of this group of voters at their peril.

Whether or not a new civil rights movement will emerge depends on the political strength, unity, and dynamism of people of color in pursuing economic and social equality. It also depends on the willingness of whites—workers and others—to reject the self-defeating logic of racial exclusion in favor of the more general logic of racial unity. The potential impact of such a movement, as the civil rights movement of the 1960s demonstrated, extends far beyond the racial order to nearly every social, economic, and political institution in America.

CHAPTER 4

Women and Children Last

Conservative economics has brought some bad news for women, as well as some not-so-bad news. The not-so-bad news is that the availability of paid employment (albeit in segregated occupations at low wages) and of government income support programs (however inadequate) has meant that women's access to income is no longer restricted to that which is redistributed to them through marriage. The bad news is that women with children but without male breadwinners are more likely than ever to be poor.

Seventy percent of the 10.7 million new jobs which opened up between 1979 and 1986 went to women. But women have not succeeded in closing the gender gap in living standards. Despite dramatic increases in the numbers of employed women, women's average income—obtained either from wages, the government, and/or husbands—relative to men's did not improve over these years.[1] Almost one million more families headed by women are below the official poverty line in 1986 than in 1979 (see Chapter 2).[2]

The increased employment of women relative to men in the paid labor market was offset, on the one hand, by cuts in the public programs on which women's and children's living standards depend; and on the other hand, by the continuing increase in the number of women whose household income is not augmented by a male paycheck. Over one-quarter of all adult women now live in such households.[3]

Conservative economic policies are not the only thing working against women and their families. There is also a distinct conservative social "gender agenda" that aims to restore the male-headed, nuclear family—usually just called *the* family—to its former prominence. The Reverend Jerry Falwell writes:

> The strength and stability of families determine the vitality and
> moral life of society. The most important function performed by

41

the family is the rearing and character formation of children, a
function it was uniquely designed to perform, and for which no
remotely adequate substitute has been found. The family is the
best and most efficient "department of health, education and welfare."[4]

Cutbacks in government health, education, and welfare programs,
especially those which support unmarried women with children, are
welcomed as a crucial strategic victory in what fundamentalist Tim La-
Haye calls "The Battle for the Family."[5]

Does the patriarchal fundamentalist agenda dovetail with conservative economic programs: high unemployment rates, high real interest rates, and the attack on organized labor? The answer, ironically, is
no. These national economic policies decimated the predominantly
male manufacturing, mining, and construction sectors, and pushed
many women into a depressed labor market. This is hardly what
Reverend Falwell had in mind.

The conservative social and economic agenda has been a
response not only to the structural crisis of the capitalist economy, but
to the crisis of the traditional family as well. Much of the support for
the conservative social agenda over the past decade has come not from
businessmen's concern with the long-term decline in profits or from
bankers' desire to restore the Almighty Dollar. Rather, its sources are
traditional ideas about what it means to be a man or a woman in our
society. Ironically, by drawing more women into the labor force, the
right-wing economic policies have done as much to challenge as to
support their preferred form of "the family."

Thus the implicit industrial policy of conservative economics—to
shift labor out of well-paid manufacturing and into lower-wage services—is on a collision course with the overt family policy of the right—
to accept no substitutes for the patriarchal family. Women and children
are caught in the middle.

• Women Hold Up Half the Economy (At Less Than Half the Price)

Many women have entered the paid labor market over the past
two decades (see Figure 4.1). If so many more women are now earning money, why has their standard of living relative to men's not improved?

Important changes in women's economic status have occurred
over the past two decades, in both access to earned income and to
governmental transfers and in-kind services. But the relative income of

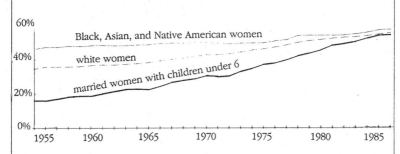

Figure 4.1

Women Enter the Labor Market

Labor Force Participation Rates of Women Sixteen Years
and Over by Marital Status and Race, 1955-1986

Source: Data on white women and on Black, Asian, and Native American women,
1955-82; from Bureau of Labor Statistics' *Employment and Training Report of the
President,* 1982, pp. 155-57, Table A-5; and various January issues of *Employment
and Earnings.* Data on married women with children under 6: BLS, *Labor Force
Statistics Derived from the Current Population Survey: A Databook,* vol. 1, Bull,
2096, Sept. 1982, p. 716, Table C-11. Data for 1983-86, *Statistical Abstract 1986,* p.
399, Table 675.

full-time female workers has shown little improvement. In 1970, women
earned 59.2 percent of what men did. That figure remained relatively
constant through the 1970s and early 1980s. By 1984, the figure inched
up to 64.3 percent, and has settled in at 65 percent in 1986. (see Figure
4.2).

Conservatives point to the increased visibility of professional
women as evidence of economic progress. While the percentage of
women in law, medical, and management professions increased between 1979 and 1986, most women remain in low-paid, "pink-collar"
job ghettos. Changes in the federal classification of occupational
categories in 1983 make long-term comparisons difficult.[6] But a look at
some detailed occupational categories shows that close to 50 percent
of all women are employed in just twenty occupations out of over 200
possibilities. The top ten occupations, which account for one-third of
all women employees, changed little between 1980 and 1986.

Between 1979 and 1986, the ratio of year-round, full-time female
to male workers' income improved for women, moving up from 59 percent to 65 percent. But this "improved" ratio is based on the relative
harm done to men's income during the recession of the early 1980s.
During this seven-year period, the real income of men fell by $892
while women's rose by $705. Virtually the entire change is attributable
to men's absolute losses suffered during the height of the Reagan-

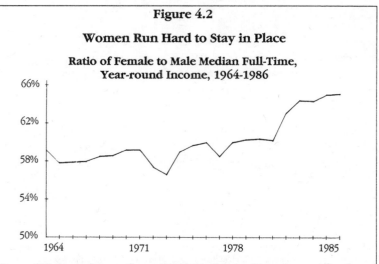

Figure 4.2

Women Run Hard to Stay in Place

Ratio of Female to Male Median Full-Time, Year-round Income, 1964-1986

Source: U.S. Census Bureau, Current Population Reports, *Money Income of Households, Families, and Persons in the U.S. 1985,* Series P-60, no. 156, Table 30, pp. 104-105. For 1986, U.S. Census Bureau, Current Population Reports, *Money Income and Poverty Status,* Series P-60, no. 157, Table 12, p. 20.

Volcker recession. Men's real income dropped $1,659 between 1979 and 1983. Women's real income rose ever so slightly—$37—over the same period. Both men's and women's incomes rebounded in the "recovery," but men's incomes have risen faster. Between 1983 and 1986, men's incomes improved $767 while women added $667 to their median incomes.[7]

The shift away from manufacturing to the service sector, described in Chapter 2, helps explain the changes in women's income relative to men's. Since women had always been locked-out of high-paying manufacturing jobs, the Reagan-Volcker recession has affected their incomes differently than it has men's. For this reason, the unprecedented rise in women's recorded income and the entry of a few women into professional and managerial positions *does not* spell generally improving living standards for women.

There is another important reason why the improved median income ratio is a deceptive measure of women's economic status. "Income" measures only earnings and government transfers, not transfers from other household earners, particularly husbands. The amount of money women actually receive in their households simply does not appear in income statistics. The dramatic change in women's marital status has reshaped women's traditional sources of income (see Figure 4.3).

To gain a more comprehensive picture, we have estimated a measure of the relative standard of living for women which takes all

Figure 4.3

Fewer Women Are Married

The Changing Composition of Households, 1950-1986

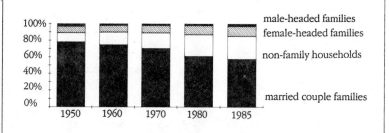

Source: Statistical Abstract, 1987, p. 42, Table 55.

income sources into account: spouses and other family members, government transfers, wages, and other income. Of course, we do not know how income is actually divided among household members. Our measure must therefore be an approximation. We measured the per capita income in all households with women and compared that to the per capita income in all households with men. We term our measure the Per capita Access to Resources or PAR (see Figure 4.4).[8]

The per capita income of women in 1985 was 87 percent of the per capita income of men. We call the difference between men's and women's income 13 points under PAR. Since 1967, the first year for which we were able to calculate the index, the amount by which women were under PAR gradually increased through the late 1970s, and has remained constant since. Between 1967 and 1985, the gap between men's and women's income has almost exactly doubled, despite the fact that the ratio of female to male incomes of full-time workers was rising.

Reduced economic dependence on men is a major gain for many women, but the monetary costs of being without a man are still high. In 1986, well over one-third of female-headed households lived below the poverty line, an increase since the late 1970s (see Chapter 2).[9] Indeed, per capita household income varies greatly with marital status. By comparison with married-couple households, the per capita income of divorced men is 53 percent greater; divorced women are 26 percent poorer; men with absent wives are 26 percent richer; and women with absent husbands are 56 percent poorer.[10]

According to the logic of conservative economics, what the

Figure 4.4

The Gender Gap in Income Widens

Women's Overall Access to Income

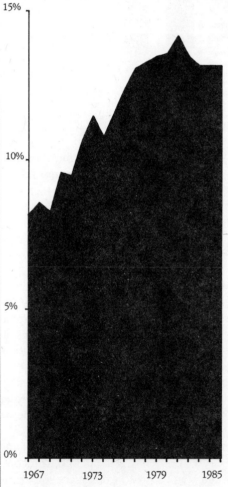

Measuring the PAR Index

The PAR index is an estimate of the average per capita income of women relative to men. To construct it, we made the hypothetical assumption that income is shared equally by all adult household members.

We first calculated the total income of married women by multiplying the number of married-couple households by their per capita income. We then calculated the income of unmarried women and other female-headed households (these include married women with absent husbands, divorced women, single women, and widows) by multiplying the number of such households by their per capita incomes. We added the two incomes together and then divided the sum by the total number of households with women in them to get the numerator of the ratio. Performing the same operation for men yields the denominator.

Source: U.S. Census Bureau, *Money Income of Households, Families, and Persons in the United States*, P-60 Series, various years.

* One minus the PAR index measures the gap between gender equality (PAR equals one) and the current reality.

market does not provide, the family will. But the market has provided women with jobs in unprecedented numbers and, partly as a result, the male-headed, single-earner family of conservative lore is a fast-fading myth. Many of the budgetary decisions and policy and legislative initiatives of the current administration can be understood as attempts to offset the increase in women's autonomy afforded by the growing demand for labor.

• Government Off Whose Backs?

Triggered by the dissolution of the male breadwinning family and the "ghettoization" of women into low-paying jobs, women's under-PAR income has been exacerbated by changes in the role and philosophy of government under the reign of the New Right. Conservatives not only identify the government as the source of all evil in the economy; they also decry government "intervention" into the family.

Embracing a political philosophy that goes beyond the New Federalism, Reagan has publicly stated his admiration for family traditionalist George Gilder, author of *Wealth and Poverty*. In his book, Gilder argues that the government—in the form of the welfare state— is responsible for the collapse of the family, as well as the stagnation of the economy. According to Gilder, income-support programs for poor and unemployed women undermine the male breadwinning role. As a result, men have lost the incentive to work and productivity has suffered. Furthermore, Gilder claims, the high taxes required to support the welfare state have caused family after-tax income to fall, driving women out of their homes and into the labor force. The male-headed nuclear family has been the casualty.

The policies that emerge from these views are clear: cut personal income taxes and slash public income support for unmarried women and their children. The advantage of unleashing the "free" market is that the economy and the family can both be taken care of by one strategy.

The stated objectives of Reagan's conservative economic policies, however, have obscured their implications for women and for family structure. Under the rubric of getting government "off our backs," conservatives have advocated not only cuts in public support geared specifically to women but cuts in domestic government spending in general. Programs for low-income families constitute less than 10 percent of federal expenditures, they sustained 30 percent of all budget cuts between 1981 and 1985.[11]

Because women and children comprise a large and increasing proportion of the poor, the primary recipients of public income-support programs are women. Indeed, the number of poor persons in female-headed households rose by 100,000 each year between the mid-1960s and the mid-1970s. According to feminist analysts Barbara Ehrenreich and Frances Fox Piven, two out of three adults living below the poverty level in 1980 were women; more than half of poor families were headed by women.[12]

Because of the increasing "feminization of poverty,"[13] the cuts in income-support and other social programs which began in 1981 disproportionately affected women. A study by the Coalition on Women and the Budget found that 94 percent of all families who received AFDC (Aid to Families with Dependent Children) payments were maintained by women (as of March 1979); 63 percent of all SSI recipients (Supplemental Security Income) were women (as of December 1981).

Ok...Ok... I'll go peacefully just so long as you leave the patriarchy in power.

credit: Chuck Segard

Moreover, Medicaid and Food Stamp recipients in 1983 were 60 percent and 85 percent female respectively, while legal services clients were 67 percent female.[14] Women of color have been particularly hard hit. In 1980, black female-headed families comprised 27.7 percent of all female-headed families but 43.4 percent of all families that were poor.[15]

Prior to the conservative strategy of cutting the federal budget in a contracting economy, income-support programs functioned precisely in reverse: to provide counter-cyclical assistance to people hurt by economic downturns. The Center on Budget and Policy Priorities estimates that if social programs had worked in this way, close to one million families would not have fallen into poverty between 1979 and 1985. In other words, 30 percent of the increase in poverty and 40 percent of the increase in numbers of female-headed families in poverty is directly attributable to conservative economic policies.[16] Cutting public support precisely at the moment when the market curtails economic opportunity, however, is the "stick" approach of conservative economics. The elimination of social welfare as a source of support "frees" large numbers of women workers for the expanding low-wage service economy.

Besides the threat of poverty, there is an added twist when the stick is applied to women. Like men, they are subject to the "discipline of the market"; unlike men, they are also subject to the discipline of the family. Reduced options, either in the labor market or in social support programs, may force women into dependence on men. Once there, if they become victims of domestic violence, they will find battered women's shelters underfunded. Even before the Reagan budget cuts, battered women's shelters across the country were forced to turn away three times the number of women they served.[17]

• Women and Children Last

A favorite target of conservative cuts in social spending programs is the AFDC program and leading the attack is Charles Murray. In his book, *Losing Ground: American Social Policy, 1950-1980,* Murray argues that AFDC reduces poor people's incentive to work (see Figure 4.5). Perhaps more than any other social program, AFDC represents an alternative—however meager—to the male-headed nuclear family for women with children.

The increased incidence of female poverty and the attack on AFDC has made "welfare reform" all the rage in Washington and in state legislatures. States must contribute to AFDC payments and have considerable leeway over types of programs and levels of funding.

Figure 4.5

Finding Scapegoats

Charles Murray's Agenda

Battered proponents of government transfer programs report that their efforts had been "Charles Murrayed."* Murray's highly influential book, *Losing Ground: American Social Policy, 1950-1980,* is a picturesquely argued case for the conservative agenda of gutting social programs. Murray argues not that the poor are more shiftless than anyone else, but that a social policy elite changed the rules by making it economically attractive for poor people to behave in ways in the short run that are destructive in the long run. Thus the various expanded social welfare programs of the 1960s and 1970s do the poor a great disservice. One of Murray's most ferocious examples concerns the AFDC program, a favorite target of other conservatives as well. According to Murray, AFDC encouraged women to shun traditional family responsibility (that is, marriage), while nonetheless allegedly persisting in having babies. In Murray's words: "The most flagrantly unrepentant seemed to be black, too." Acccording to Murray, AFDC did not reduce poverty. Rather it ensured that millions of poor children would never grow up with first-hand experience of the virtues of hard work. Murray compares total real federal cash expenditures on public assistance with the number of persons below the poverty line from 1950 to 1980, and concluded that increased assistance caused increased poverty.

This conclusion is very odd in view of the fact that poverty rates and government transfers—revealed in Murray's own figures—unmistakably move in opposite directions.** One could use these data to make a stronger *prima facie* case for the opposite assertion: that public assistance reduced poverty, and when transfers were cut, poverty began to rise.

Murray contends that rising transfers for the poor induced most reasonable people within the reach of eligibility to abandon work and embrace idleness. Since the major alternatives to wage work for most women are housework and childcare, Murray's assumption of carefree leisure is highly suspect. Existing research has found a small wage work disincentive in AFDC. As demeaning as AFDC recipients know it to be, it does provide an alternative—or more often, a supplement—to the most underpaid and degrading jobs.

AFDC may have contributed to some of the rise in female-headed households until the 1970s but the increase in participation is more likely due to the welfare rights movement which made program eligibility more visible to the poor.**** In any event, in the 1970s, real per capita AFDC benefits shrank under inflationary pressure. AFDC families as a percentage of all female-headed families also fell, while the extent of female household headship continued to set new records each year.

* *Newsweek,* February 1, 1985.
** *Ibid.,* p. 18.
*** *Ibid.., p. 57.*
**** Frances Fox Piven and Richard A. Cloward, "The Contemporary Relief Debate," *The Mean Season,* Fred Block, Richard A. Cloward, Barbara Ehrenreich, and Frances Fox Piven, New York, Pantheon Books, 1987.

However, most of the state programs—with Massachusetts' "Employment and Training Choices" program in the lead—and the federal program proposed by Senator Daniel Patrick Moynihan (D-NY) are policies which put the poor to work, increase child support compliance, but do not call for significant increases in funding.[18]

On the surface, these programs seem to make political and fiscal sense. But not too much scratching reveals they are avoiding the real problems related to the causes of poverty among female-headed households. First, women raising children are already working—but not for pay. More importantly, the jobs women get do not lift them and their families out of poverty, especially when the cost of childcare and health care are included in the cost of living. In 1986, the poverty threshold for a family of three was $8,737. The median income for a woman in the same year was $7,610 and the yearly earnings for a person working full-time, year-round at a minimum wage job were $6,978.[19]

Insistence that fathers pick up the welfare tab instead of the government is not likely to work either. A large portion of men—particularly young men—do not pay child support because they cannot afford to. The recession and decline in manufacturing jobs have caused the earnings of men aged 20-24 to fall by 30 percent from 1973 through 1984. This has meant fewer men can support families, no matter how stringent the child support enforcement laws become. In 1973, 60 percent of all 20-24 year old men earned enough to support a family of three above the poverty level; by 1984, only 42 percent could.[20] More importantly, the trend away from marriage is so strong and striking that a policy which tries to enforce "father-rule" seems antiquated at best.

The welfare reform debates and other conservative policies concerning women's poverty rest on the assumption that childbearing and childrearing are private, not social, responsibilities. But the labor and material costs of raising children are disproportionately borne by women.[21] Resorting to "old-fashioned" support mechanisms for mothers and children does not hold out much promise.

It is unlikely that the long-term trend toward non-marriage will be reversed and an increasing number of children will therefore grow up in female-headed households. Since children put a dent into female income which is already at poverty level or below, it is not surprising that the economic welfare of such households depends primarily on the age and number of children within them. Economist Nancy Folbre has termed this phenomenon "the pauperization of motherhood."[22]

Like public support to the elderly, public inter-generational transfers of income to children comprise part of government responsibility in most other industrialized countries. Indeed, according to a recent study, the United States does less to relieve the private costs of rearing children than any of the other industrialized countries.[23]

Government income support for children, which often takes the form of child welfare allowances, reflects the reality that childrearing is not only work but work that is important to the long-term health of

the economy. Indeed, childrearing may be considered the most important of all long-term economic investments. Yet, it is labor which goes
unpaid.

Available information suggests that the amount of time women
spend doing unpaid work is falling, but that their total work week
(waged and unwaged work) is rising. The bulk of necessary work at
home is still left up to women. Victor Fuchs estimated that women per-
formed 70 percent of all "non-market" work in 1979.[24] Women provide
30-40 percent of all wage work and 70 percent of all unwaged work;
yet the ratio of average income of all women with income relative to
that of all men with income in 1986 was 44 percent.[25] In other words,
it is likely that women do over half of all the work that gets done in
this country and continue to make less than half of what men do.

• The New Double Standard

Our contention that conservative economics is about family policy
as well as economic policy helps to explain aspects that otherwise appear to be contradictory. The 1985 *Economic Report of the President,*
for example, emphasized a reduced role for the federal government in
all aspects of the economy. In particular, it supported deregulation,
competition, and free choice. Reagan administration officials who have
objected to government interference in the "free" labor market to over-
come sexual and racial discrimination have also objected to the
proposal that all work of comparable value to employers be paid equally. Indeed, Clarence Pendleton, head of the U.S. Civil Rights Commission, called comparable worth the "looniest idea since loony tunes."[26]

According to a report in *Business Week,* if women today earned even three-quarters of what men did, the country's total wage bill would be an additional $100 billion.[27] That means that discrimination cost every employed woman $2,123.38 in 1984.[28] It is clear that what is meant by the "market solution" is the continuation of depressed wages for women because discrimination is part of the marketplace.

Furthermore, so committed are conservatives to the workings of the existing "free" market that they have reduced government support for programs that help women compete in the market. The Women's Educational Equity Act, funded at $10 million in 1981, was cut to $5.8 million in 1984, and was slated to receive no funds at all in the proposed FY1986 budget.[29]

The President, who campaigned against the Equal Rights Amendment on the grounds that adequate legislation against sex discrimination already exists, has curtailed enforcement of those laws. Reagan's Justice Department has also changed the standard by which discrimination can be said to exist. According to an Urban Institute Report, court decisions in the years prior to 1981 held that the effects of apparent discrimination (e.g. under-representation of women in a particular firm's pattern of promotion), were sufficient cause to order a remedy. The current Justice Department standard requires the more stringent proof of *intent* to discriminate.[30] As a result, the Equal Employment Opportunity Commission (EEOC) failed to find violations in 40 percent of all new complaints filed in 1984; the figure for 1981 was 23 percent.[31] Federal outlays for enforcement of equal opportunity statutes have also declined. Between FY1981 and FY1983, the EEOC saw its budget cut by 10 percent in real terms and its staff by 12 percent. The EEOC is authorized to initiate litigation against discriminators. Between 1981 and 1983 there was a 60 percent decline in lawsuits filed by the Commission.[32]

Ironically, an administration which campaigned on the platform of getting the government off the backs of the American people and out of the economy has attempted to legislate the most private aspects of people's lives. The conservative attack on abortion, gay and lesbian rights, and family planning is directed at controlling people's—especially women's—sexual decisions. Eliminating access to abortion is prominent among President Reagan's social policy goals. Conservatives have gone so far as to support a so-called Human Life Amendment to the U.S. Constitution. The New Right aims to overturn the *Roe v. Wade* Supreme Court decision (1973) which ruled that a woman's decision to end a pregnancy was a fundamental right to privacy protected by the 14th Amendment.

• Impoverished Freedoms

The changing relationship of family, economy, and government in the United States today has not opened up new vistas of economic opportunity and personal choice for women; it has closed them down. Continuing labor market discrimination and cutbacks in income support programs leave many women with little choice but to endure unwanted marriages, exchanging their autonomy for their livelihood.

To improve women's and children's living standards and to make individual choice about family structure a reality, public policy must move in three directions: (1) it must increase women's employment opportunities and remuneration; (2) it must provide adequate public support for the work of childrearing; and (3) it must provide adequate income support programs. As long as childrearing is devalued, as long as discrimination persists in labor markets, women will share unequally in social income and their personal liberty will be constrained.

Establishing greater social responsibility for children and their caretakers through government is a high priority for reducing women's and children's poverty and involves a major reorientation in the relationship between state and family. By way of comparison, an enormous change in the relationship between government and the private economy was necessary to address the record levels of unemployment in the Great Depression. After World War II, tremendous headway was made in reducing unemployment because the government made a commitment to moderate the effect of the business cycle. Likewise, poverty among the elderly was reduced because the government committed itself to transfers through the Social Security system. Something on the same order is now necessary to contend with the social challenge of female-headed families.

Women and men are increasingly choosing non-traditional family structures: many are single, many will pass through one or more marriages, many live in collectives, many are part of lesbian and gay couples. Allowing a wide and broadening range of family choices must be a central tenet of any society which calls itself democratic. Neither the market nor the traditional family—the two pillars of conservative thought and social policy—will secure this liberty; indeed, we have suggested that they constitute obstacles to broadening the range of choices facing women and men.

Without active government intervention in markets to combat discrimination, without the recognition of childraising as socially valued work worthy of social remuneration, and without the establishment of an adequate income floor, the freedom to choose will remain an illusion for most—and for many, an impoverished freedom.

• **Chapter 2**

1. *Wall Street Journal*, "Reagan Team Weighs Impact of Welfare Cuts on Working Parents," October 21, 1981, p. 1; George E. Peterson, "Federalism and the States," in John L. Palmer and Isabel V. Sawhill, eds., *The Reagan Record*, The Urban Institute, Ballinger, Cambridge, 1984, p. 232.

2. James Fallows, "America's Changing Economic Landscape," *Atlantic*, March 1985; Paul O. Flaim and Ellen Sehgal, "Displaced Workers of 1979-1983: How Well Have They Fared?," *Monthly Labor Review*, Vol. 108, No. 6, 1985, pp. 3-16.

3. U.S. Census Bureau, Current Population Reports, *Money Income and Poverty Status of Families and Persons in the United States: 1986* (Advanced Data), P-60 Series, July 1987, No. 157.

4. U.S. Census Bureau, Current Population Reports, *Money Income of Households, Families, and Persons in the United States: 1985*, P-60 Series, August 1987, No. 156, Table 3.

5. In 1986, 6,943 of the 12,876 children below the poverty level lived in female-headed households. U.S. Census Bureau, July 1987, *op. cit.*, Tables 16 and 18.

6. *Economic Report of the President, 1987*, Table B-26, calculated in 1986 constant dollars.

7. The unemployment rate for blacks aged twenty and over was 12.9 percent for men and 12.4 percent for women in 1986. *Economic Report of the President, 1987*, Table B-38, p. 288.

8. The Federal Reserve's survey of consumer finances, which includes unrelated individuals as well as families, shows comparable aggregate trends.

9. U.S. Census Bureau, July 1987, *op. cit.*, Table 4.

10. *Federal Reserve Bulletin*, "Survey of Consumer Finances, 1983: A Second Report," December 1984, pp. 863-864. Financial assets are checking, savings, NOW and money market accounts, certificates of deposit, IRA or Keogh accounts, savings bonds, stocks, bonds, nontaxable holdings, and trusts. Financial assets do not include property and businesses.

11. In 1986 the poverty rate was 17.6 percent higher than in 1979 and 23.7 percent higher than in 1973. U.S. Census Bureau, July 1987, *op. cit.*, Table 16.

12. In 1983, the infant mortality rate declined by 2.6 percent from the 1982 rate. Between 1972 and 1982, the annual average rate of decline was 4.6 percent. See Mickey Leland, "For America's Poorest, Infant Mortality is Up," *The New York Times*, October 24, 1985.

13. C. Arden Miller, "Infant Mortality in the U.S.," *Scientific America*, July 1985, pp. 31-37.

14. Mickey Leland, *op. cit.*
15. *Ibid.* The 1983 rate for whites was 9.7 per 1,000 live births; for blacks the rate was 19.2 per 1,000.
16. C. Arden Miller et. al., "The World Economic Crisis and the Children: United States Case Study," *International Journal of Health Services*, Vol. 15, No. 1, 1985, p. 127.
17. Prime-age men's share of the unemployment rate was 56.7 percent and prime-age women's was 23.6 percent from 1975-1982 (cyclical troughs). Moreover, involuntary job loss increased unemployment rates between 1969 and 1982, while voluntary quits made a declining contribution to unemployment, and labor force entrants had a basically constant effect on unemployment over this period. Michael Podgursky, "Sources of Secular Increases in the Unemployment Rate, 1969-1982," *Monthly Labor Review*, July 1984.
18. Dooley and Gottschalk asserted that "a decline in the trend toward greater inequality within education-experience categories is not strongly confirmed by the data for men with more than 10 years of experience." Michael Dooley and Peter Gottschalk, "Does a Younger Male Labor Force Mean Greater Earnings Inequality?," *Monthly Labor Review*, November 1982, p. 43. In a later study, Dooley and Gottschalk found that the proportion of men with weekly earnings below $231 (in 1984 prices) rose from 12.3 percent in 1969 to 13.4 percent in 1973 and to 15.2 percent in 1978, the last year for which their data are available. See "The Increasing Proportion of Men With Low Earnings in the United States," *Demography*, Vol. 2, No. 1, February 1985, pp. 25-34.
19. U.S. Census Bureau, *Household and Family Characteristics: March 1985*, Series P-20, September 1986, No. 411.
20. Mary Jo Bane, "Household Composition and Poverty," in Sheldon H. Danziger and Daniel H. Weinberg, eds., *Fighting Poverty: What Works and What Doesn't*, Cambridge, Harvard University Press, 1986, p. 214.
21. Elaine McCrate, "The Growth of Nonmarriage Among U.S. Women: An Unanswered Question for the New Family Economics and an Alternative," Mimeo, University of Massachusetts, 1984, p. 2.
22. Average gross hourly earnings, total private non-agricultural labor force, *Economic Report of the President, 1987*, Table B-41.
23. Barry Bluestone and Bennett Harrison, *The Deindustrialization of America*, Basic Books, New York, 1982, p. 26.
24. Candee S. Harris, "Plant Closings: The Magnitude of the Problem." Working Paper 13, Business MicroData Project, The Brookings Institution, Washington, D.C., June 1985.
25. Flaim and Sehgal, *op. cit.*
26. This figure actually understates the length of time without work because many workers surveyed were still unemployed in January 1984.
27. Flaim and Sehgal, *op. cit.*
28. Louis Jacobson, "Earnings Losses of Workers Displaced From Manufacturing Industries," in W. C. Dewald, ed., *The Impact of International Trade and Investment on Employment*, U.S. Department of Labor, Bureau of International Affairs, Government Printing Office, 1978.

29. Steelworkers Research Project, *Chicago Steelworkers: The Cost of Unemployment*, Local 65, United Steelworkers of America, 1985, p. 16.

30. *Ibid.*, p. 22.

31. Peter Henle and Paul Ryscavage, "The Distribution of Earned Income Among Men and Women, 1958-1977," *Monthly Labor Review*, April 1980, pp. 3-10. The last year for which information is available is 1977.

32. Robert D. Plotnick, "Trends in Male Earnings Inequality," *Southern Economic Journal*, January 1982, pp. 724-732.

33. Henle and Ryscavage, *op. cit.* Neither of these studies included workers with no earnings at all. However, Dooley and Gottschalk (*op. cit.*) found that the proportion of men with zero earnings increased from 1967-1978, even within groups having the same education and experience.

34. Sara Kuhn and Barry Bluestone, "Economic Restructuring and the Female Labor Market: The Impact of Industrial Change on Women," paper presented to the Conference on Women and Structural Transformation: The Crisis of Work and Family Life, Rutgers University, November 1983. Direct production employment in key manufacturing industries is declining absolutely as well as relatively. Kuhn and Bluestone estimated that total production employment in manufacturing fell 5 percent from 1973-1980. Ten key industries lost 1.3 million jobs from 1972-1982. In the 1983-1984 recovery, twenty-nine of the seventy-four major manufacturing sectors continued to decline, while twenty-eight others had 1984 employment levels significantly below 1978 levels. These industries, which provide almost 75 percent of manufacturing employment, lost 1.9 million jobs since the 1983-1985 recovery began.

35. For data on other developed economies, see *Labor Force Statistics 1958-1979*, OECD, 1981 and *Yearbook of Labour Statistics*, ILO, 1980, 1982.

36. Jack Carlson and Hugh Graham, *The Economic Importance of Exports to the United States*, Center for Strategic and International Studies, Georgetown University, Washington, D.C., 1980, p. 20.

37. Joseph A. Peckman and Mark J. Mazur, "The Rich, The Poor, and the Taxes They Pay: An Update," Brookings General Series Reprint 409, The Brookings Institution, Washington, D.C., 1985, p. 34.

38. Sheldon Danziger and Peter Gottschalk, "The Poverty of Losing Ground," *Challenge*, May-June 1985, pp. 32-38; and "Macroeconomic Conditions, Income Transfers, and the Trend in Poverty," in D. Lee Bawden, ed., *The Social Contract Revisited*, Washington, D.C., 1984.

39. Marilyn Moon and Isabel Sawhill, "Family Incomes: Gainers and Losers," in Palmer and Sawhill, eds., *op. cit.*, p. 329.

40. Danziger and Gottschalk, in Bawden, ed., *op. cit.*

• Chapter 3

1. "People of color" refers to all ethno-racial groups. We do not use "minorities" because the numerical connotation suggests that discrepancies in social status, political power, and/or wealth are primarily the result of population differences. In many regions and urban areas, a racial group or groups form

the majority, yet they remain second-class citizens. Power and wealth, in short, are simply not proportional to numbers.

2. Michael Reich, "Postwar Racial Income Differences: Trends and Theories," Mimeo, University of California, Berkeley, 1985.

3. Sheldon Goldman, "Reorganizing the Judiciary: The First Term Appointments," *Judicature*, Vol. 68, Nos. 9-10, April-May 1985, p. 319.

4. "Decline Found in Proportion of Blacks in Medical Schools," *The New York Times*, October 10, 1985. The study was published in the October 1985 issue of *New England Medical Journal*.

5. William K. Stevens, "Black and Standard English Held Diverging More," *The New York Times*, March 15, 1985.

6. Edward B. Fiske, "Minority Enrollment in Colleges Is Declining," *The New York Times*, October 27, 1985.

7. *Economic Report of the President, 1974*, pp. 151-152.

8. Peter Bohmer, "The Impact of Public Sector Employment on Racial Inequality: 1950-1984," unpublished dissertation, University of Massachusetts, Amherst, 1985, pp. 34-42.

9. U.S. Census Bureau, Special Studies. *The Social and Economic Status of the Black Population in the United States*, P-23 Series, No. 80, p. 74.

10. Non-white is a Census Bureau category describing people of color.

11. U.S. Census Bureau, Current Population Reports, *Money Income of Households, Families, and Persons in the United States*, various years. Reich finds that in urban areas outside the South, the median income of black males relative to white males fell considerably from .73 in 1949 to .67 in 1979. By this measure, virtually all northern cities comprised more racially discriminatory environments in 1979 than they had three decades earlier. (Reich, *op. cit.*)

12. Randy Albelda, "Black and White Women Workers in the Post-World War II Period," unpublished dissertation, University of Massachusetts, Amherst, 1983, p. 26.

13. U.S. Department of Labor, "Employment and Earnings Characteristics of Families, Second Quarter 1985," No. 85-337, August 21, 1985.

14. Bohmer, *op. cit.*, pp. 246-247. The adverse trend in the black unemployment rates over the period 1976-1984 is a departure from the earlier period in which a weak trend of improvement existed for men and no discernable trend existed for women. The post-1975 adverse trend for both men and women is highly significant statistically.

15. U.S. Department of Labor, Bureau of Labor Statistics, *Handbook of Labor Statistics*, 1980, Table 26.

16. Southwest Voter Registration Project, "Growing Problems in a Growing Community," Washington, D.C., 1984; and Center on Budget and Policy Priorities, "Falling Behind," Washington, D.C., 1984.

17. Center on Budget and Policy Priorities, *op. cit.*

18. Lenneal J. Henderson, "Blacks, Budgets, and Taxes: Assessing the Impact of Budget Deficit Reduction and Tax Reform on Blacks," *The State of Black America*, National Urban League, New York, 1987.

19. Henderson, *op. cit.*

20. Henderson, *op. cit.*, p. 80.

21. The marginal tax rate is the rate a taxpayer pays on one more dollar of income.

22. *Economic Report of the President, 1980*, p. 80.

23. See Defense Budget Project, "Fiscal Year 1986 Defense Budget, The Weapons Build-up Continues," Center on Budget and Policy Priorities, Washington, D.C., April 1985.

24. The Congressional Budget Office estimates insignificant differences in the increased economic activity caused by the spinoff effects generated from military spending relative to those of other government programs. Critics, however, maintain that multiplier effects are lower and that military spending generates net job losses. See Robert W. DeGrasse, *Military Expansion, Economic Decline*, Council on Economic Priorities, New York, 1983; David McFadden and James Wake, *The Freeze Economy*, Mid-Pennsylvania Conversion Project, Mountain View, California and National Clearinghouse, Nuclear Weapons Freeze Campaign, St. Louis, Missouri, 1983; and William D. Hartung, "The Economic Consequences of a Nuclear Freeze," Council on Economic Priorities, New York, 1984.

25. It comes at the expense of expenditures in military personnel (which will shrink from 28.6 percent in 1980 to 22.8 percent in 1986), and operations and maintenance (which will be reduced from 32.2 percent to 25.6 percent). Defense Budget Project, *op. cit.*

26. Calculated from Bohmer, *op. cit.*, Table 23.

27. Bohmer, *Ibid.*, pp. 260-262.

28. Jonathan Leonard, "What Was Affirmative Action?," *American Economic Review*, May 1986, pp. 359-363.

29. In the Weber case—mandating separate lists for selecting candidates for training programs—only four blacks were hired in a plant of 300 employees. The effect of the Fullilone case—requiring a 10 percent set-aside in construction contracts—accounted for .25 percent of total construction expenditures. Finally, the Bakke case, although it banned quotas, reaffirmed favorable consideration of race as a factor in university admissions. Nonetheless, most universities only target people of color as a small fraction of their total enrollment. Herman Schwartz, "Affirmative Action," *Minority Report*, L.W. Dunbar, ed., New York, Pantheon Books, 1984, pp. 58-75.

30. Robert Pear, "Rewriting Nation's Civil Rights Policy," *The New York Times*, October 7, 1985.

31. These estimates ignore the Latino population in order to simplify calculations. The assumption of differences in wages mostly as a result of wage discrimination depends on equal levels of productivity for white and black workers. For the plausibility of this argument, see Omer Galle, Candace Wiswell, and Jeffery Burr, "Racial Mix and Industrial Productivity," *American Sociological Review*, Vol. 50, 1985, pp. 20-33. See also Victor Perlo with Gordon Welty, "The Political Economy of Racism and the Current Score," in Marvin Berlowitz and Ronald Edari, *Racism and the Denial of Human Rights*, Minneapolis, MEP Publications, 1984; and Lester Thurow, *Poverty and Discrimination*, The Brookings Institution, 1969.

32. The evidence is examined in Michael Reich, *Racial Inequality*, Princeton, Princeton University Press, 1981.

33. Kenneth M. Dolbeare, *Democracy at Risk: The Politics of Economic Renewal,* Chatham House, New Jersey, 1984, Table 11.5.

• Chapter 4

1. See Figure 4.3 which presents our calculations of women's income relative to men's.

2. U.S. Census Bureau, Current Population Survey, *Money Income and Poverty Status of Families and Persons in the United States: 1986 (Advanced Data),* July 1987, P-60 Series, No. 157, Table 16.

3. In 1986, 28 percent of all households were female-headed. *Ibid.,* Table 14.

4. Reverend Jerry Falwell, *The Fundamentalist Phenomenon: The Resurgence of Conservative Christianity,* Doubleday, New York, 1981, p. 206.

5. Tim LaHaye, *The Battle for the Family,* Fleming H. Revell Company.

6. Nancy F. Rytina and Suzanne M. Bianchi document these changes in *Monthly Labor Review,* March 1984, Vol. 107, No. 2, pp. 11-17.

7. All numbers for year-round, full-time incomes are in 1986 dollars. U.S. Census Bureau, *Money Income of Households, Families, and Persons in the United States: 1985,* August 1987, P-60 Series, No. 156; and U.S. Census Bureau, July 1987, *op. cit.*

8. The measure does not take account of taxes or in-kind transfers of any sort.

9. In 1986, 34.5 percent of all female-headed families were below the poverty line compared to 30.4 percent in 1979. U.S. Census Bureau, *Characteristics of the Population Below the Poverty Level: 1984,* P-60 Series, June 1986, No. 152; and U.S. Census Bureau, July 1987, *op. cit.*

10. U.S. Census Bureau, August 1987, *op. cit.,* Table 4.

11. Center on Budget and Policy Priorities, *End Results: The Impact of Federal Policies Since 1980 on Low Income Americans,* Washington, D.C., 1984.

12. Barbara Ehrenreich and Francis Fox Piven, "The Feminization of Poverty: When the Family Wage System Breaks Down," *Dissent,* Spring 1984, p. 162.

13. Diana Pearce coined the term in "Women, Work and Welfare: The Feminization of Poverty," in Karen Volk Feinstein, ed., *Working Women and Their Families,* Sage Publications, London, 1979.

14. Coalition for Women and the Budget, *Inequality of Sacrifice,* National Women's Law Center, Washington, D.C., 1984. Food Stamps recipients include women and children combined. Women also constituted more than 50 percent of social security recipients. This program, however, was not severely trimmed back.

15. Catherine L. Hammond, "Not Always 'Just a Husband Away From Poverty': Race, Class, and the Feminization of Poverty," Mimeo, University of Massachusetts, Amherst, 1982, p. 25.

16. Center on Budget and Policy Priorities, *Impact of Government Anti-Poverty Programs Declines,* November 1986.

17. Coalition on Women and the Budget, *op. cit.*

18. For an overview of the programs at the state level see "The Retreat From Welfare," *Dollars and Sense,* No. 127, June 1987, pp. 6-8.

19. U.S. Census Bureau, July 1987, pp. 38, 20.

20. Cliff Johnson and Andrew Sum, "Declining Earnings of Young Men," Children's Defense Fund, May 1987.
21. Nancy Folbre, "The Pauperization of Motherhood: Patriarchy and Public Policy in the U.S.," *Review of Radical Political Economics*, Vol. 16, No. 4, 1985. While social conservatives like Gilder suggest that women shoulder the burden because welfare payments have undermined the traditional family, there is evidence that even within male-headed families, the work of rearing children falls disproportionately on women.
22. *Ibid.*
23. Alfred J. Kahn and Shelia B. Kamerman, "Income Maintenance, Wages, and Family Income," *Public Welfare*, Fall 1983.
24. Victor R. Fuchs, "His and Hers: Gender Differences in Work and Income, 1959-1979," Working Paper No. 1501, National Bureau of Economic Research, 1984.
25. U.S. Census Bureau, July 1987, *op. cit.*
26. *The New York Times*, November 17, 1984, p. 15.
27. *Business Week*, January 28, 1985, p. 81.
28. Calculated from a total female labor force of 47,095,000 in 1982. *Statistical Abstract of the United States 1984*, p. 413.
29. Coalition on Women and the Budget, *op. cit.*, p. 51.
30. John L. Palmer and Isabel V. Sawhill, *The Reagan Record*, The Urban Institute, Washington, D.C., 1984, p. 206.
31. Coalition on Women and the Budget, *op. cit.*, p. 51.
32. Palmer and Sawhill, *op. cit.*

ABOUT THE AUTHORS

Randy Albelda is the general editor and project coordinator of *Mink Coats Don't Trickle Down*, author of Chapter 1, and co-author of Chapter 4. She is currently the research director of the Massachusetts State Legislature's Special Commission on Tax Reform. She is a collective member of the monthly economics journal *Dollars and Sense* and a member of the Economic Literacy Project of Women for Economic Justice in Boston. Randy received her Ph.D. in economics from the University of Massachusetts in 1983. She is a co-editor of *Alternatives to Economic Orthodoxy: A Reader in Political Economy* (M.E. Sharpe, 1987) and has published in *Industrial and Labor Relations Review, Socialist Review,* and the *Review of Radical Political Economics.*

Elaine McCrate is the author of Chapter 2. She is an assistant professor of economics at the University of Vermont. Elaine is currently working on a post-doctorate degree at the Afro-American Studies Program at the University of California, Los Angeles, examining the relation between work, educational opportunities, and teenage pregnancy. Elaine received her Ph.D. from the University of Massachusetts in 1985. She has published in the *American Economic Review*, the *Review of Radical Political Economics,* and the *Boston Globe.* Elaine has been active in the women's movement since 1972.

Edwin Meléndez is the author of Chapter 3. He holds a Ph.D. in economics from the University of Massachusetts and is an assistant professor in the Department of Urban Studies and Planning at the Massachusetts Institute of Technology. He is formerly an organizer and activist in the Puerto Rican student and labor movements. Edwin has also taught economics and Puerto Rican Studies at Fordham University. He is the author of a major econometric model of the Puerto Rican economy in the post-World War II period. He is currently conducting research on income inequality and labor force participation among ethno-racial groups in Boston and New York City.

June Lapidus is co-author of Chapter 4. She is a doctoral candidate in economics at the University of Massachusetts and has taught women's studies at the State University of New York, Buffalo. Her current research is on temporary workers in the U.S. economy. June has published in *Feminist Studies*, the *Review of Radical Political Economics*, and (along with Albelda and McCrate) is working on research which examines the economic status of women in the postwar period.

The Center for Popular Economics was founded in 1979 to train public interest, community, women's, labor, religious, peace, gay and lesbian, and third world groups in economic concepts and issues. The Center's workshops, Summer Institute, and publications demystify economics and give social change advocates an integrated overview of current economic issues. In addition to the *The Economic Report of the People* (from which this book is derived, South End Press, 1986), the Center has also published *A Field Guide to the U.S. Economy* (Pantheon, 1988).

For more information on the Center's programs, contact:
Center for Popular Economics, Box 785, Amherst, MA, 01004
(413) 545-0743.